*Standing in the
Education Gap*

Standing in the Education Gap

A Commonsense Approach to Helping Your Child Succeed in School

MARC LAPOINTE

iUniverse LLC
Bloomington

Standing in the Education Gap
A Commonsense Approach to Helping Your Child Succeed in School

Copyright © 2013 Marc Lapointe.

All rights reserved. No part of this book may be used or reproduced by any means, graphic, electronic, or mechanical, including photocopying, recording, taping or by any information storage retrieval system without the written permission of the publisher except in the case of brief quotations embodied in critical articles and reviews.

iUniverse books may be ordered through booksellers or by contacting:

iUniverse
1663 Liberty Drive
Bloomington, IN 47403
www.iuniverse.com
1-800-Authors (1-800-288-4677)

Because of the dynamic nature of the Internet, any web addresses or links contained in this book may have changed since publication and may no longer be valid. The views expressed in this work are solely those of the author and do not necessarily reflect the views of the publisher, and the publisher hereby disclaims any responsibility for them.

Any people depicted in stock imagery provided by Thinkstock are models, and such images are being used for illustrative purposes only.

Certain stock imagery © Thinkstock.

ISBN: 978-1-4917-0120-1 (sc)
ISBN: 978-1-4917-0122-5 (hc)
ISBN: 978-1-4917-0121-8 (e)

Library of Congress Control Number: 2013913684

Printed in the United States of America.

iUniverse rev. date: 8/26/2013

To my beautiful wife, Cindy: While I'm busy writing about how to properly educate students, you're living it out every day with our kids.

To Ethan and Makaila, whose excitement for this project sometimes surpassed my own.

Special thanks to my father and mother, who encouraged me to write this book in the first place, and to Angi and Clayton – I asked for your two cents' worth—and it turned out to be gold.

Contents

Preface ix
Introduction xiii
Part 1: Cutting Through the Noise 1
- Chapter 1: Self-Esteem in Our Schools 3
- Chapter 2: Lifting the Veil 25
- Chapter 3: The Vagueness of the Curriculum 39
- Chapter 4: Learning Through Discovery 53
- Chapter 5: Individual Learning Styles 71

Part 2: Moving Forward 85
- Chapter 6: Math: The Right Formula 87
- Chapter 7: Understanding Reading 111
- Chapter 8: The Skill of Learning 131
- Chapter 9: The Habits and Routines of Successful Students 149
- Chapter 10: The Intangibles 163

Part 3: Educating Your Child at Home 179
- Chapter 11: The Growing Appeal of Homeschooling 181

Part 4: Outside Help 199
- Chapter 12: Why Look for Outside Help? 201

Conclusion: Let Common Sense Be Your Guide 217
Notes 221
Index 227
About the Author 239

Preface

MY INVOLVEMENT IN EDUCATION HAS spanned two decades. At the beginning of my career—armed with a heart for teaching kids, a brain full of fresh ideas and a graduate degree in education—my aim was to transform young, eager minds into enthusiastic and innovative lifelong learners. My role as a teacher, I believed, was to teach kids to think critically, solve complex problems and grow in knowledge. Idealistic, I know. Yet years later, I would say that my aspirations for young people are still the same and perhaps even greater. What has changed, however, are the means by which I believe I, and all other educators and parents, should work toward achieving those goals.

There's a lot of "noise" in education—meaning that between so-called experts, special-interest groups, government agencies, administrators and teachers, there are endless opinions on how best to teach our kids. Some of it is sound advice, but a lot of it makes little sense. Much of it can be confusing. I learned this very early in my teaching career. In fact, red flags starting going up for me while I was still in graduate school. But like many new and eager teachers, I simply chalked up my concerns to inexperience.

As the years went by and I become a veteran teacher, my concerns didn't fade. In fact, I began to realize that many of the ideas involved in teaching—philosophies, methods, resources and so on—didn't make a whole lot of sense. I wasn't the only teacher who felt that way, but it became clear that those of us who voiced such concerns would be derided for not being more progressive.

It took a while for me to reach the conclusions I have about effectively educating our children. I would say that it's the uniqueness of my experiences as an educator that led me to write this book. When I say "unique," I don't necessarily mean exceptional, just different. I didn't begin my career as a teacher, nor has my entire career in education been strictly as a classroom teacher. I have had the opportunity to observe education from many perspectives—as a graduate student, as a classroom teacher, as a businessman and as a father.

Not until I founded Acumen Education did I begin to sort through the noise and come to a more comprehensive understanding of why, in general, our kids struggle as students and our schools fall short of thoroughly educating them. When I became involved in the tutoring industry almost a decade ago, my sole goal was to establish a successful business while using the experience and expertise I gained in my years of teaching. But not long after my tutoring company was up and running, it became very apparent that all was not as it should be in elementary education and beyond.

Acumen Education and, more specifically, my role within it evolved. How could it not? I couldn't ignore what I was witnessing: kids with dwindling skills in math, reading and writing and an education system that was selling them short. Over the years, I've not only talked to a lot of parents to understand the source of their frustration, but I've met with numerous teachers and education experts to try to get a pulse on where and why our schools are falling short. Over time, Acumen became more than just a tutoring service: it was an information hub. Parents were calling to get answers about a whole range of issues related to elementary education. Quite simply, they were seeking honest answers about how they could help their children become better students.

This book, in large part, is my response to those questions and concerns. While I'm certainly critical of various aspects of our education system in these pages, my goal is to go beyond mere criticism. What I really want to offer here is something that parents can use: insight into our education system and practical advice on how, as parents, we can make a difference in our children's education. The challenge in writing this kind of a book isn't in the amount of information that I can share, but in scaling it back. My goal is to give guidance that's simple and straightforward. When I say "simple," I don't mean dumbed down. Instead, I mean that it involves the one resource available to all parents: common sense. I talk a lot about common sense as the essential ingredient in helping our kids become better students and, by extension, better educated.

That means that more than any teacher, coach, peer or anyone else your child may develop a relationship with during his or her time in school, your involvement as a parent is crucial. I'm not suggesting that anyone else, particularly teachers, can't have a major influence in your child's life and even inspire your son or daughter. But under normal circumstances, no one has a more influential presence or a greater emotional investment in your child than you, the parent. As you get deeper into this book, my hope is that you will feel empowered by what you read. But even more importantly, my wish is that those parents who are concerned about the quality of their children's education will find the information, advice and encouragement they need to make a real difference for their sons and daughters.

Introduction

"How can my child become a better student?"

In all my years as an educator, this question, by far, is the one that parents have asked me the most. It really only scratches the surface of parents' real concerns. They want more than just good grades for their kids (although good grades are important). They want their children to be truly *educated*—to learn and master academic skills, to become knowledgeable and skilled, to be engaged in learning even outside of school and to have the ability and drive to pursue a successful and satisfying career one day.

Our schools provide an immeasurably valuable service. There are few things as noble and worthwhile as educating children. Yet schools fall short. It's alarming how many children enter high school without having the most fundamental and basic skills in math, reading and writing. Of course, this isn't true of every young student, but this negative trend is so obvious that it shouldn't be ignored. Which brings us back to our original question: How can your child become a better student? If you want your child to be the type of student who not only earns good grades but masters foundational skills and concepts with confidence, is appropriately self-sufficient and learns how to interact with others, then there is only one answer: your involvement as a parent.

Now, while your role in your child's education is vital, it doesn't have to be a massive undertaking. In fact, I believe it's the little things that parents do that can have the most dramatic effects. Malcolm Gladwell describes this process in his book *The Tipping Point*:

In the end, Tipping Points are a reaffirmation of the potential for change and the power of intelligent action. Look at the world around you. It may seem like an immovable, implacable place. It is not. With the slightest push—in just the right place—it can be tipped.[1]

The tipping points, as Gladwell describes them, are not one-time, dramatic moments. They are small and sometimes barely noticeable actions that come together to eventually cause a big and lasting change. While Gladwell's book mainly revolves around the world of business, his theory can also apply to our efforts as parents to help our kids become great students. It's the small things you do at home with your child that will, together, over time, make the biggest and most profound difference in her education.

That's my ultimate aim with this book: To show you, as a parent, how you can make a big difference in your child's education through "intelligent actions," however small. Above all else, I believe parents can be a tremendous help to their kids if they arm themselves with a simple but essential tool, and that is common sense. Unfortunately, as you'll see, for all the impressive ideas, theories and methods proposed by our system of education, a discouraging few are actually based on common sense.

Before we go any further, let me explain what I mean by "common sense," especially as it pertains to your child's education. The Merriam-Webster Dictionary defines common sense as "sound and prudent judgment based on a simple perception of the situation or facts."[2] Now, if we take this formal definition and apply it to the realm of education, we can say that it's a philosophy of teaching that is based on approaches that are observable and actually work for the majority of students in a realistic scenario, not on unproven ideas or methods that sound good but are impractical in their application and desired outcomes.

In elementary education in particular, many of the theories on effective teaching and learning are not rooted in the observable realities of the classroom. So, in other words, while many of the current ideas in education may have value for certain individuals—typically those who already have a degree of knowledge and experience—they simply don't make sense for the majority of young students who have yet to accumulate a necessary body of knowledge, skill and experience. What this means for parents is that, regardless of the complexity that seems to shroud the realm of elementary education, they can bring about the most dramatic and lasting changes in their child's learning simply by following the approaches, routines and habits that have been demonstrated to be the most effective means by which kids can learn.

With all of this in mind, I believe it's critical for parents to understand exactly what ideas in education dominate the average classroom. That's why Section 1 of this book deals primarily with the most common (and questionable) philosophies and teaching approaches found in our education system, in an attempt to demonstrate why they are largely ineffective and, therefore, make little sense. You'll discover that much of what is proclaimed as best practices in teaching is, in fact, based on assumptive reasoning. Put another way, it's simply *assumed* by many teachers and parents that a certain philosophy or approach to teaching is the right way because it's so widely advocated, regardless of the practical implications and negative outcomes. Not only will you fully grasp the challenges to your child's learning, the first section essentially lays the foundation for Section 2, where I detail the practical steps you can follow to provide real and effective help for your child.

Allow me to be clear on what this book is *not* about. It's not about how you, the parent, can lobby for positive change within our system of education. Certainly some of the topics discussed will cast a critical eye on the way things are done in the classroom and with the curriculum. As you read, the need for change, while understated, will be obvious. There are plenty of newspaper editorials, academic papers and books written on the need for change and how it should be done. The reality is that this has been going on for decades, so it's clear that real, effective change moves slowly in the realm of education.

This book is about the need for parents to get involved in their children's education. In particular, it's for those who have children in elementary school, since much of what is learned from kindergarten through Grade 8 provides the foundation for success in high school and university. My hope is that, by reading these pages, you will not only come to fully grasp just how important you, as a parent, are to your child's academic success, but also realize that the help you provide doesn't have to be complicated and time-consuming to be valuable.

Many parents who are concerned and frustrated feel too unsure of what to do to take action. Usually this uncertainty comes from a feeling that, as parents, we aren't trained to teach and we don't understand the intricacies of the curriculum or the standards and learning outcomes. We put a great deal of faith in our schools and believe that, even if our children struggle now, they will one day, somehow, catch up or simply "get it." Unfortunately, this is rarely the case, and our hesitation and indecision will only make things worse for our kids.

When I speak about being involved in your child's education, I'm not talking about attending parent-organization meetings, volunteering in the classroom or chaperoning field trips. While these activities all have value and allow you to build rapport with the teachers and school administration, it's not the sort of participation that gets you directly involved in your child's learning. Being an involved parent means teaching, reinforcing and keeping your child accountable as a student. We'll not only observe what goes on in our schools, we'll look closely at the things that are essential for elementary students to learn and master and how parents can ensure that their kids do learn them. We'll also take a look at how parents can make best use of outside help to assist or complement their efforts if need arises.

I think it's important to be clear about one other thing: I'm not taking aim at teachers. There is a tendency, I've discovered, for parents armed with the kind of information they'll glean from these pages to challenge the expertise and even the motivation of their children's teachers. There are many teachers who recognize the problems within our education system and work tirelessly to ensure their students are successful in spite of those problems. These teachers are invaluable, but they can only work within the circumstances they're given. They need our support, not our derision.

A word of warning before we move forward: If you wish to see real, positive and lasting change in your child's academics, you must be committed and patient. Too often, in a world that demands immediate results, parents are treated to the illusion that their children's grades can be improved dramatically and for the long term in a few short weeks thanks to any number of learning centres, tutoring services or pre-packaged math and reading programs. Unfortunately, in many cases, even if some children make short-term progress through such programs, it's quickly lost and forgotten because the underlying challenges remain.

Don't be fooled when other parents or teachers suggest that, given enough time and maturity, your child will eventually catch up. While time and maturity certainly help, knowledge and skills don't develop by themselves. The longer you wait for this well-intentioned but misinformed piece of advice to take effect, the greater your child's struggles will become.

PART 1

Cutting Through the Noise

TIME AND AGAIN I CHAT with parents who know that their children are struggling in school. They often talk about intervening in some way, but quickly convince themselves that, at some point, their children's school will solve the problem. After all, we trust that teachers are rigorously trained, that the curriculum is specific and carefully mapped-out, that our kids are building upon valuable knowledge and skills year after year, and that current teaching methods are tried and true.

As we begin to examine how we can become effectively involved as parents, it's important to examine our system of education with a critical eye. Understanding the fundamental challenges within our schools is the first step toward helping your child improve as a student. In this section, we'll take a closer look at the self-esteem movement and how it has permeated almost every aspect of the elementary-school environment. We'll also take a closer look at the assumptions we make regarding schools in general and shed some light on what is really going on. Finally, we'll scrutinize popular teaching methods and the theories that go hand in hand with them.

As you'll see, our education system is full of ideas and theories that sound good on paper, but often lack careful forethought, planning and common sense. Our schools are constantly seeking ways to improve the classroom environment and the ways in which students are taught, so you can hardly blame educators for attempting to devise new approaches and methods that might bring about positive change. The problem is that our kids become guinea pigs. More often than not, ideas that sound good are either not properly tested and observed or are taken too far.

While some of the things you learn may surprise and frustrate you, remember that we're talking about the culture of education in North America in general. In other words, much of what you'll discover in these pages is true of most of our elementary schools at one level or another. However, there are schools, administrators and teachers that buck the trend and teach not according to popular trends in education but with common sense. So this section is also meant to help you appreciate the overwhelming pressure our teachers and administrators are under to conform to often unproven, untried and unreasonable teaching methodology.

By the time you've finished reading through this first section, you should understand the need for your involvement on a much deeper level. While you may already have the sense that something is not quite right in our schools, you will have the knowledge to move forward with certainty and confidence.

CHAPTER 1

Self-Esteem in Our Schools

OURS IS A CULTURE THAT is fixated on self-esteem. Bookstores are filled with self-help books and magazines are chock-full of articles on how to obtain a better self-image. Positive self-esteem is seen as the gateway to a more successful and fulfilling life and is the prescription for all sorts of social and behavioural ills. This, naturally, spills over into parenting and education. So obsessed are we with promoting positive self-esteem in our kids that we look to shelter them from anything that could possibly threaten their confidence and self-image. If we're not careful, we can easily lose sight of what is truly important for our kids, particularly in the area of education.

The movement to build our children's self-esteem has been gaining steam for years. It's been observed and written about for more than three decades. The irony is that, despite years of ineffective teaching approaches and curriculum modifications, the self-esteem movement within the North American system of education is stronger than ever. Even more perplexing are studies that reveal, time after time, that efforts to put the self-esteem of each child first, before academic performance, are at best inconclusive and at worst actually harmful.

It's important to point out that self-esteem, particularly in children, isn't a bad thing. On the contrary, kids with greater self-esteem tend to be more self-sufficient, have positive social skills and feel motivated to excel in many areas of life. As parents, haven't we seen over and over again that a little confidence goes a long way in motivating and inspiring our kids? Self-esteem shouldn't be confused with arrogance, since arrogance has little to do with having a reasonable amount of confidence but, instead, is typically more about overblown pride and a puffed-up and unrealistic self-image. The issue, therefore, isn't with building up the self-esteem of our kids, but with the way in which our culture and our schools encourage us to go about it.

The self-esteem movement is a perfect example of an idea that has been taken too far. The problem, as you'll see, isn't with raising kids to be confident, it's the idea that we must do all that we can, even in the face of failure, to make sure students "feel good" about themselves. It has little, if anything, to do with real accomplishments, effort or hard work. In fact, within our schools, our children are being taught that success has nothing to do with performance—it's based on nothing at all but ensuring that we don't injure a child's self-esteem.

The Allure of Self-Esteem

Why have our schools put the self-esteem of students ahead of academic performance? While there are a number of possible explanations, there are four beliefs in the power of self-esteem that are most pervasive. At first glance, they seem to make perfect sense. Time and again we are told stories of children who, having been made to feel good about themselves and their abilities, achieve great success and recognition. Even in the lives of our own kids we notice that, with enough encouragement, they can overcome any number of obstacles. However, within our education system, we have largely ignored other measures of success and progress in favour of measuring a child's level of self-esteem.

Belief #1: Our Children Are Special

As parents, we want our children to know they are loved, to discover their talents, to have opportunities to pursue their interests, to be good people and, most importantly, to be happy. While our goal is to instruct and guide, we are also instinctively protective and naturally do what we can to keep them from being hurt or discouraged. School in particular is a place rife with challenges. We worry about our children being accepted by their peers, developing an interest in learning and ultimately succeeding in their academics. The thought that our children could become discouraged or frustrated by any lack of success can cause us a great deal of anxiety.

It brings great joy to parents when they see their children happy and confident. It should go without saying that poor grades, frustration and a feeling of inferiority do little to make a child feel happy or confident. Over the past 30 years, in response to parents' desire to ensure their children feel anything but frustrated and discouraged, educators have moved toward ensuring that classrooms are places where children may develop positive self-esteem and steering away from anything that could threaten that self-esteem.

Belief #2: Self-Esteem = Better Students

Ask almost any classroom teacher what he or she believes is the greatest intangible that students should have for academic success, and most often, you'll be told that it's confidence. When a student experiences success, she is more confident; when she has confidence, she is motivated and much more likely to grasp new concepts and experience more success. If we look into our own lives, we can see exactly how this works. We tend to be interested in things that we are relatively good at, and as a consequence, we have greater confidence in that area.

Since self-esteem is very much connected to confidence, and confidence is associated with greater motivation and, ultimately, success, educators see it as the ultimate tool. The question, then, is how to instil and maintain positive self-esteem? Within our schools, the solution has been to create a learning environment that discourages competition, highlights the individual learning styles of children and avoids objective assessment and evaluation. In this way, children no longer have to fear failure or even mediocrity and, the thinking goes, avoid the inevitable damage that would be done to their self-esteem. Our desire to help our children build confidence, while a good goal, has been taken too far. The result? Any threat to a child's confidence and sense of self-worth is viewed as detrimental and to be avoided at all cost.

Belief #3: Self-Esteem = Positive Behaviour

Teaching in the elementary classroom involves a great deal of classroom management. There are so many variables in a classroom containing anywhere from 20 to 35 students, and good teachers find ways to manage this setting so that, as much as possible, all of the students can benefit. Within any classroom, behavioural issues crop up from time to time. Poor or disrespectful behaviour among one or many of the students can cause severe disruptions and ultimately rob other students of the opportunity to learn.

Self-esteem is often viewed as the "silver bullet" to solving behavioural issues within a classroom. The theory goes something like this: A student who consistently misbehaves has low self-esteem or, at the very least, a complete lack of confidence when it comes to academics. Naturally, when a child lacks confidence, her tendency is to draw attention away—through disruptive behaviour—from the fact that she doesn't grasp the material. If a teacher could somehow boost her self-esteem, the student would likely become much more interested in school, participate in a positive way and experience greater motivation. This, in turn, would lead to better overall behaviour and, ultimately, a much more positive learning environment for all of the students.

Belief #4: Self-Esteem = Greater Tolerance

Bullying and intolerance are hot issues in North American society today. Great emphasis has been placed on finding ways to counter bullying in schools and teach students the merits of accepting other beliefs, cultures and lifestyle choices. Self-esteem, as in the case of classroom behaviour, is seen as the ultimate solution to the problem of bullying and intolerance. It's widely believed that students with low self-esteem are the greatest cause of bullying and intolerance.

Whether parents like it or not, schools have become as much about teaching children socially acceptable behaviour as they are about teaching academics. It shouldn't come as a surprise, since within the average classroom are students from a variety of cultural and even religious backgrounds. Tolerance is necessary not only for a cohesive learning environment but for acceptance outside of the classroom. What better place to teach this concept than within the classroom? While tolerance in and of itself is a good thing, it is the belief that self-esteem leads to greater tolerance and, therefore, less bullying that is questionable. This only serves to put a greater focus on self-esteem— rather than core subject knowledge—as a mandate within our schools.

The Reality of Self-Esteem

For all of the apparent virtues of self-esteem as a means of increasing student learning and achievement, it has fallen far short of its intended goals. American education expert Jeanne S. Chall explains this in her book *The Academic Achievement Challenge*:

> While one can appreciate that self-esteem is a worthy goal in itself, a considerable amount of research and past experience suggests that pursuing it as a means of raising achievement levels will be in an incomplete solution, at best.[3]

Yet, in spite of experience and research to the contrary, the self-esteem movement within our schools is not only alive and well, it has come to actually dominate the curriculum. It's baffling that such a notion could hold such sway simply because it *feels* right. What has resulted is both frustrating and disturbing.

Lowered Expectations

Years ago, as a relatively new teacher, I noticed a disturbing trend. More and more students were entering their grade-eight year unable to multiply simple numbers, successfully complete a long-division question or, in a troubling number of cases, subtract two-digit numbers. What I discovered was that more and more teachers, from the primary grades onward, were allowing their students to use calculators. Baffled, I chatted with my colleagues, some of who were allowing students to use calculators for simple calculations. I was told that it was too much to expect that all of their students could master these basic math skills. It took too much time, it intimidated too many students, and it left some feeling inferior and inadequate. The solution? Use a calculator.

Back then I had little idea that the self-esteem movement in our classrooms was becoming so influential. Today I encounter so many instances of dumbing down or lowered expectations that it's almost rare to find classrooms where high expectations and standards are the norm. Calculators instead of memorizing the times tables or working problems out on paper; "free writing" instead of grammar and punctuation; a whole-language reading approach instead of phonics—these are just a few examples of how we have replaced techniques that actually work with approaches where students can experience success with little or no effort. The new definition of success in these cases doesn't amount to learning, however good the students may feel about themselves.

Sometimes learning requires hard work, time and perseverance. It may mean that a student occasionally struggles or even fails at an assignment or task. Our response to these challenges shouldn't be to lower our expectations. If a child struggles with long division or writes a paragraph full of spelling and grammatical errors, the worst thing to do is to give the student free use of a calculator or turn a blind eye to poor writing. Instead, we should set a high but achievable academic standard for our kids. We are mistaken if we believe that setting the bar low will actually build a child's self-esteem in the long run. We shouldn't shy away from the idea that, at times, a young student may experience some setbacks or even failure. The key is to provide the kind of guidance and assistance that will teach a child to overcome failure or wrestle through a setback so that, when she is successful, it will be the kind of accomplishment that builds real confidence, persistence and perspective.

Watered-Down Assessments

Objective measures to assess what a child has learned, such as tests and quizzes, are becoming more and more rare. This isn't to say that young students are never tested, but that this type of evaluation takes a back seat to more "progressive" methods of grading. It's argued that strict, objective testing can be a source of great anxiety for many students—which, besides increasing overall stress levels, makes students who perform poorly feel inferior to their peers—and so this kind of assessment should be avoided. Things like portfolios, projects, peer feedback and self-assessments have become the norm. In addition, it's common for many teachers to give retests, give credit for corrections or provide some other method of evaluation that ensures that a child's final grade will end up being a positive one.

As we'll examine in a later chapter, giving students opportunities to complete projects and to show off their particular learning preferences is of great importance and there's nothing wrong with evaluating a student's knowledge and progress through methods other than traditional tests and exams. However, these more progressive methods are, in many cases, becoming the only measures used. Less traditional and more creative means of assessment and evaluation can have real value, but too often the grading criteria are ambiguous and subjective.

Instead of carefully worded rubrics that describe in precise, subjective language the requirements, expectations and measurements for grading for things like presentations, writing assignments or portfolios, we often see a numerical system, perhaps from one to five. The assignment may be evaluated on a number of aspects, such as breadth of information, creativity and so on. The teacher then circles the number, or grade, that he or she deems appropriate for the corresponding "criteria." Certainly a teacher may have a general sense of what a student deserves, but this leaves far too much room for subjectivity and comparison with other assignments.

Grading and assessment can even change from one year to the next within the classroom of the same teacher. It's not unusual for some teachers to grade more rigorously one year and less the next, according to the perceived collective ability of his or her students with each new class. This likely means that we wouldn't necessarily notice a difference from year to year between the number of higher and lower grades because the standard would change according to the overall "ability" of the class. With each class of students that passes through each year, teachers can make sure that the overall success rate doesn't severely dip but remains more or less the same—or improves.

Without methods of evaluation that are consistent and objective regardless of the perceived abilities of the classroom as a whole, this problem will persist. Grades should never be a reflection of how a student did in comparison to her classmates or how that class compared to another from the year before; they should hold to a specific and unchanging standard. If our goal is to truly educate students, grading on a curve or a sliding scale will do little to accomplish this. When grading follows a fixed standard, teachers and parents are better able to understand exactly where a child needs improvement and help. Are we really doing our kids any favours when the work they've produced is "good enough" in comparison to their peers? Has real learning actually taken place when we can't say, with any certainty, what a child has or hasn't mastered?

Vague Report Cards

For many elementary students, particularly from kindergarten through Grade 3, letter grades have been completely replaced. Report cards either contain lengthy comments from the teacher or contain standard phrases like "not yet meeting expectations," "meeting expectations" and "exceeding expectations." Even report cards that contain letter grades are most often accompanied by ambiguous teacher comments that are vague when it comes to areas of concern but are full of encouragement and praise for areas of perceived strength.

An article in the *Globe and Mail* entitled "Canadian Parents Give Reports a Failing Grade" sums up the shortcomings of elementary-school report cards: "They [the parents] yearn for information on how to help their child get ahead, but report cards rarely deliver."[4] Instead of receiving documents that give a fair, objective evaluation of a child's progress and areas of need, parents are instead stuck with lines of unclear edu-babble that are short on concrete and helpful information. For many teachers, it's better to avoid any hint of criticism in order to ensure that a child feels good about her progress. Just as vital, teachers want to avoid any confrontations with parents who believe their child deserves better.

Effort Over Performance

Within our schools, effort has, in large part, been deemed more important than performance. In other words, educators are much more concerned about a child's level of effort than whether or not she experienced real success. On the surface, this sounds like a positive step, since success or good grades don't always come even when a young student tries hard. This can lead to a good deal of discouragement when, even though the student works hard at something, the results don't match the effort. As parents, this can be a frustrating dilemma, particularly as we try to help our frustrated child make sense of this seemingly unsolvable puzzle.

While effort is an important component of academic success,

placing such a high degree of importance and focus on a child's effort at the expense of actual results can be detrimental. Effort is relative. What one person might consider time-consuming and laborious may be somewhat easy for the next. It typically depends on a person's work ethic, experience and level of knowledge and skill. I have worked with numerous young students who feel that investing anything more than 45 minutes of study time on an upcoming test represents tremendous effort. I have also observed students, particularly those who have been raised in cultures outside of North America, who think nothing of devoting several hours of time to their studies each day.

Effort for its own sake doesn't necessarily mean that a child's time is being used wisely and efficiently. I frequently encounter young students who tell me that no matter how hard they try they always perform poorly on math tests. I then press to find out exactly how these struggling math students are actually using their study time. I'm often told that they will spend hours studying for a math test the night before. While the time may seem gruelling, I'll ask these students why they cram the night before. Why not begin studying a week ahead of the test date and commit 30 minutes each night to studying? To these students, such a solution seems implausible. They either don't want to sacrifice 30 minutes of their time for six or seven nights or feel that so little time per session just doesn't seem like hard work. My next question usually revolves around how a student uses her time. Does she complete numerous practice questions to the point where she would be able to answer any math question without hesitation? The answer, most often, is no. Instead, many students choose to stare at their math texts, making mental checklists. On occasion, if a concept or procedure appears tough to grasp, they *might* complete a practice question or two. Are these students working hard? Certainly. Are they working efficiently? No.

Valuing effort over results ultimately leads to mediocrity. The theory goes that as long as a student tries hard, well, that's what really counts. If we choose not to hold our students to a certain standard—one based on results—then we take away their opportunity to learn from mistakes and find out how to work better, not just harder. Working better is itself a skill that can be learned and is invaluable in high school and university. A focus on effort leads to a downward spiral. Students may work "hard," but results are mediocre. So we lower our standards to the point where they learn very little, are satisfied with mediocrity and always expect credit for merely trying hard. There is little, if any, common sense in awarding high grades for mediocre work, regardless of effort.

Inflated Grades

Few things make a child as happy or a parent as proud as when the child brings home a great grade on an assignment or a test. Any child who has worked hard for that success deserves to feel that she has truly accomplished something. The problem, however, is that the growing trend in schools across North America is higher grades for students completing less work. We may be tempted to view this as a positive sign for today's students—more kids achieving greater academic success—but while grades may be way up on average, actual learning is being severely compromised.

In Canada, the Canadian University Survey Consortium (CUSC) discovered that over 70 percent of first-year university students reported having an A- average or better in high school.[5] Twenty years earlier, in the 1980s, only 40 percent of students reported having such a high average. That's a significant increase. Such massive leaps are similarly reported in the United States. Do we assume that today's high-school students are more studious, harder working or more intelligent than those of 20 year ago? It is no coincidence that, with an ever-increasing focus on sensitivity to student self-esteem, average grades have increased significantly. Some would argue that, in fact, it's because students have greater self-esteem that they have enjoyed academic success. However, this apparent success doesn't always translate into success in university.

Out of all the students surveyed in 2010, after having time to adjust to the academic rigours of university life, only 30 percent expected to achieve an A- average or better. In fact, only 25 percent reported having had very much success in their first year in university. According to the CUSC, "students' perceived lack of success in this regard may relate to the fact that, for many, their grades are less than what they might have expected." Of course, it isn't unusual for first-year university students to experience some relative struggles as they adjust to the routines and expectations of university life. However, the gap between expectations and reality is impossible to ignore.

Perhaps even more revealing is undergraduate students' perception of grading in university. In a recent study published in the journal *Active Learning in Higher Education*, it was found that undergraduate students believed that 39 percent of their grade should be based on effort and 61 percent on actual performance.[6] The study goes on to state that "findings appear to suggest that students judge professors as unfair when the perceived effort invested in the completion of an assignment does not compensate for actual poor performance."[7] How can students possibly be convinced that almost 40 percent of their grade should be based on effort? How can effort even be graded? In her book *The Feel-Good Curriculum*, Maureen Stout addresses this difficulty:

> Since there is no way to accurately measure effort, students can claim they did the best they can, and

we will never know if it is true or not. And of course suggesting that they didn't is a hazardous policy, since if it turns out that they really did do their best, both teacher and student end up feeling pretty bad. Finally, students figure out pretty quickly just how they can manipulate the system for their own ends.[8]

Effort is subjective and impossible to quantify. Besides, in the real world, it isn't how hard someone tries that amounts to success; it's the results. When in need of a vital service like surgery, who would choose the doctor who tries hard but gets few positive results over the doctor who actually gets results?

We shouldn't be surprised that today's university students have these attitudes since they have been rewarded for effort and mediocre performance since the primary grades. Inflating grades in elementary and high school in the name of self-esteem leads students to feel more entitled. They may believe that their grades have been earned, but we sacrifice real learning and positive performance and severely hamper their ability to translate real effort into real success.

Social Promotion

The vast majority of public school boards and private schools have a no-fail policy. This means that no matter how a child performs academically, she will be promoted to the next grade. Since being held back can be emotionally distressing for a child, it's viewed as far more damaging than allowing her to move forward even if she hasn't shown that she has the knowledge and skills necessary for the next grade. Holding back a child, the theory goes, would only intensify her academic struggles; the social stigma would be so great that learning would never take place. Once again, positive self-esteem is the ultimate goal.

Standing in the Education Gap

Social promotion is, at best, a short-term solution. While we may save a young student from the perceived embarrassment of being held back while her peers move on to the next grade, all we really end up doing is reducing her chances of academic success in the years to come. There is little to be gained and much more to be lost academically. When we advance students who are in no way ready for the next grade, not only do we risk further decline in their learning, but we also end up creating feelings of inferiority and a lack of self-confidence anyway. Imagine a student who can't grasp a math lesson because she hasn't learned the basic concepts from the previous grade or cowers from class discussions because she barely grasped similar material from the year before.

In reality, as many studies have demonstrated, there is no clear advantage to retention or social promotion if circumstances don't change. Without some kind of effective intervention, a child will likely continue to struggle in school whether she has been held back or not. The best kind of intervention, then, comes from parents. Even if it can't be clearly shown that retention is more beneficial than allowing a struggling student to advance, social promotion is a precarious policy simply because it can cause parents to feel that everything is okay or, with time, any academic issues will take care of themselves.

Another problem with social promotion is that it places a tremendous amount of the burden on teachers, particularly those who teach intermediate and higher elementary grades. Chall explains this problem:

> Social promotion has also meant that the teacher, in grades beyond the first or second, has the difficult task of teaching a class with students who vary widely in achievement. This variation grows with each successive grade and becomes more onerous for the teacher.[9]

When the expectation is for teachers to effectively teach a class of 20 to 35 students in an integrated classroom and pay particular attention to the various "learning styles," the end result is diluted expectations and standards.

The Fallout

We've seen how the self-esteem movement in our schools has had an effect on standards and expectations. Just as important, and disturbing, is the effect it has on the character of our children. In *Generation Me,* psychologist Jean M. Twenge describes modern children this way: "Today's young people are experiencing that society right now, and they speak the language of the self as their native tongue. The individual has always come first, and feeling good about yourself has always been a primary virtue."[10] Yet for all the importance placed on self-esteem and its apparent virtues, the results have been far more detrimental than our society cares to admit.

Can't Accept Criticism

In the name of positive self-esteem, our children are subjected to an environment of unconditional validation. Nothing they do is considered "not good enough." There is no unacceptable or low standard of performance and outcomes are always positive. When we focus on building a child's self-esteem at all costs, we create individuals who not only can't understand their own shortcomings, but also are unable to take any form of criticism and use it to improve in areas of deficiency. Twenge makes the following observations:

One downside to this generation is that they don't take criticism well. The self-esteem ethos in schools and parenting has valued protecting young people's positive self-feelings over all else. Some Gen Me'ers attended schools where teachers did not correct their mistakes, and others had parents who let them do whatever they wanted. They are used to feeling important and having their work praised. [11]

For students to experience real learning and, ultimately, real success, they must have the ability to continuously strive for improvement and excellence. Yet teachers are encouraged to only highlight what is positive—even when a child's performance is clearly inadequate and there's little to be positive about. Criticism, particularly when it's meant to be constructive and helpful, should be a normal part of a child's education. If a young student can't complete a long-division question, is it better to ignore this gap in her learning and, instead, pat her on the back for the effort? Or is it far more important to point out that it was wrong and teach her how to do it correctly?

If educators withhold their criticism, failing to point out where and how a student can improve, they ultimately take away a child's ability and desire to improve and strive for excellence. I'm not suggesting that we shouldn't also point out what they've done well and provide ample encouragement, but we must stop treating students as though their feelings, and ultimately their sense of self-worth, are as fragile as crystal. One of our greatest goals for our kids is for them to grow up to become successful at whatever they choose to do. We must remember that academic success is the means, not the end goal.

We should always be careful to balance our constructive criticism with a child's feelings. It's important not to confuse constructive criticism with negative, harmful criticism. While we may be critical of the unbalanced methods of the self-esteem movement, we mustn't fall into the trap of going to the other extreme. Constantly pointing out where a child can improve with little or no regard for her effort can indeed impair a child's confidence and ability to cope. If we can find the right balance we'll better equip kids not only for success in school but also for success in any career or endeavour long after their years in school are over.

Inflated Self-View

In our all-out desire to ensure that kids feel special, we run the risk of producing students with an inflated view of themselves that can lead to a sense of undue entitlement. It's an attitude of self-importance in which a student feels unrestricted and finds issue not with her own shortcomings, but with the shortcomings and "unfairness" of others.

There is a great deal of focus in our elementary schools on building a child's sense of self-importance. Twenge observes that "many school districts across the country have specific programs designed to increase children's self-esteem, most of which build self-importance and narcissism." She goes on to point out that

> Even programs not specifically focused on self-esteem often place the utmost value on children's self-feelings. Children in some schools sing songs with lyrics like "Who I am makes a difference and all our dreams can come true" and "We are beautiful, magnificent, courageous, outrageous, and great!" Other students pen a "Me Poem" or write a mock TV "commercial" advertising themselves and their good qualities.[12]

While self-esteem may not be promoted in the same way in

every school, the message is clear: Our children are taught that they are special and that they should focus on what makes them special before all else.

To be sure, it's important that we show children that they are indeed special regardless of how they stack up to others. The issue, however, is teaching children to focus so much on themselves, to feel so much self-importance, that they come to expect that others will see them, and therefore their desires, as the most important thing in the world. In the classroom, this manifests itself in many ways. You can see it particularly in the grades kids receive. If it's a poor grade, the student won't see that as her fault but more likely the fault of the teacher.

When students develop inflated views of themselves, anything that falls short of their expectations is unfair and, therefore, must be fixed to suit their expectations. This attitude can carry on through high school and even university. Stout, a university professor, describes similar encounters with university students as she began her postsecondary teaching career:

> Students began trickling in to my office with the same comments and demands: I need a better grade. I deserve an A on this paper. I *never* get B's.... Along with those who clearly believed that they were entitled to an A, there were those who didn't think they needed to do any work and exhibited considerable surprise when they consequently failed the class.[13]

Clearly, the only thing we are really teaching students when we place such an emphasis on self-esteem is that they somehow deserve good grades. The irony is that while our system of education speaks of producing students who develop a "love for learning," we end up fostering the opposite. True learning consists of constantly seeking to learn, to grow and to improve.

An inflated self-view replaces true learning with a sense of entitlement. After all, if a student feels that she's owed something, particularly an unearned high grade, then there is no room for learning.

Inability to Persevere

When self-esteem becomes the means by which we help students learn and succeed, we end up creating a classroom environment in which students expect—and receive—positive and almost immediate gratification. When effort is considered more important than outcomes and no project or assignment is ever considered to be substandard, the average student comes to expect a positive remark and a good grade every time. When we take a look back at the university statistic cited earlier in this chapter, it's no wonder that so many first-year college students are overwhelmed.

We look to our schools, at least in part, to develop positive character traits in our children. Our schools, in turn, look to create a place for positive character development through value statements and philosophical ideals that are meant to remind staff of their mission and to encourage students in their goals and values. We hear or read about so many schools being places of positive community, where every individual has value. They may even speak of a positive learning community where character matters above all else. But they seldom speak of instilling perseverance in their students.

Perseverance is the ability to continue an activity or to work toward a goal through challenges and even occasional failure. It's a character quality that allows a person to recognize her own faults or mistakes and improve on them in order to accomplish her goals. Perseverance helps a person to become more patient, determined and tenacious. It's one of the most important characteristics that can help struggling students become strong, enthusiastic and successful learners. Yet because self-esteem is deemed most important, students never have the opportunity to develop perseverance. In fact, in the name of self-esteem, the opposite happens: Students avoid challenges, expect rewards for a minimal amount of work and seldom learn patience or tenacity.

Real Self-Esteem

The belief that self-esteem is the precursor of academic success is, flatly, a myth. Accomplishments—real accomplishments that have come about through challenge, hard work, perseverance and even some failure, are the pathway to positive self-esteem. In "Students Need Challenges, Not Easy Success," published in the journal *Educational Leadership*, educational psychologist Margaret M. Clifford makes the following observation:

> It is only success at moderately difficult or truly challenging tasks that we explain in terms of personal effort, well-chosen strategies, and ability, and these explanations give rise to feelings of pride, competence, determination, satisfaction, persistence, and personal control. Even very young children show a preference for tasks that are just a bit beyond their ability.[14]

By placing so much importance on self-esteem, we have done a great disservice to our children. Such a focus is short-sighted and fails to consider the long-term implications for their academic success as well as their character development. There is no question that we should always encourage our children, but there is a difference between ensuring children feel good about themselves and encouraging them. Encouragement is not about saying things that make a child feel good (although it may be sometimes), it's about helping a child to recognize her strengths and weaknesses and providing her with skills and tools that will allow her to utilize her strengths and strengthen her weaknesses.

Common sense tells us that real accomplishments—ones based on authentic results—lead to greater confidence. Artificially puffing up a child's sense of self-worth, while a very enticing idea, ultimately works against her ability and desire to truly learn. Common sense also tells us that doing the complete opposite, being constantly critical, is also a bad idea. We can, and should, have high expectations of our children, particularly when it comes to their academics. Having a high standard, though, requires encouragement and recognition for effort and progress. We must accept, and have our children recognize, that effort requires time, perseverance and the occasional setback. The ultimate goal is for our children to become satisfied not with effort alone, but with what their effort can ultimately produce: results.

CHAPTER 2

Lifting the Veil

MOST PARENTS ENTRUST THEIR CHILDREN'S education and overall academic development to the school. We assume that our children will learn about math, language arts, social studies, science and so on within the confines of the classroom setting. We hope that our children will build positive friendships and learn the value of teamwork, effort, inclusion and other social values. In some cases, parents may choose to send their children to a private school that is more in line with their own religious beliefs or perceived educational standards.

Here in North America, we're very fortunate to have such easy and open access to public education. There are tens of thousands of hard-working teachers and administrators who dedicate themselves to educating our children. We have come to expect quite a bit from our education system, and as a consequence we have made assumptions—many of them false ones—about the ability of our schools to adequately educate our children on their own.

Even as a graduate student, it was apparent to me that not everything parents believed about our system of education was entirely accurate. In my years as a classroom teacher and, later, as an education consultant, it became impossible to ignore the gap between what we assume as parents and the actual realities of the classroom. After years of observing, researching, talking with classroom teachers and administrators and hearing from many frustrated parents, I've compiled a catalogue of the most common beliefs we have as parents, why we have them and what is actually going on.

Assumption #1
Teaching, and Therefore Learning, Has Advanced Since We Were Kids

I have met with a lot of parents who are under the impression that teaching methods and resources have "advanced" since they were in school. With great leaps in the amount and kinds of technology available coupled with easy access to unprecedented amounts of information and communication through the Internet, it would be natural to assume that classroom learning is superior to that of a generation ago. It's true that, compared with the type of information and technology available to teachers as little as a decade ago, the opportunities to present information in new and interesting ways has never been greater. Yet Mark Bauerlein, in his book *The Dumbest Generation*, observes that

> … in sum, while the world has provided them extraordinary chances to gain knowledge and improve their reading/writing skills, not to mention offering financial incentives to do so, young Americans today are no more learned or skilful than their predecessors, no more knowledgeable, fluent, up-to-date, or inquisitive, except in the materials of youth culture. They don't know any more history or civics, economics or science, literature or current events. They read less on their own, both books and newspapers, and

you would have to canvass a lot of college English instructors and employers before you found one who said that they compose better paragraphs. In fact, their technology skills fall well short of the common claim, too, especially when they must apply them to research and workplace tasks.[15]

So often we hear about reforms in education, the promises of the latest and greatest texts and resources, the integration of technology and new and innovative approaches to teaching. In the end, it all amounts to very little, if any, actual advancement in the education of our children. While it's certainly important that educators constantly strive to improve on the way they educate their students, the greatest error in our education system is its tendency to completely throw out current approaches and resources in favour of completely new ones. Seldom do education "experts" examine what is currently working or how to use traditional methods to complement new ideas. Instead, a new idea or theory is wholeheartedly adopted and, with very little experimentation or consultation, exalted as the best and only way to teach elementary students… until the next great idea comes along.

"Discovery" learning is one example of this kind of thinking. While we will discuss the implications of this in much greater detail in a later chapter, the bottom line is that, currently in our elementary schools, learning through rote memorization and practice and other more traditional teaching approaches is greatly discouraged. Instead of providing students with the foundational skills needed to engage in more complex, higher-order skills, a discovery approach places far greater emphasis on mastering concepts and not procedures. The result is more and more students advancing through school without basic and essential writing or math skills.

Assumption #2
Teachers Are Experts in All Subject Areas

This is a common assumption made particularly of elementary school teachers. We believe that, since an individual has received a degree, engaged in a practical development program and received a teaching certificate that he or she must have specific training in each subject area. Unfortunately, this is just not the case. While it's certainly true that, for many elementary grades, most of the subjects are manageable for most teachers, the reality is that they don't receive subject-specific training while in their teacher-training program.

This raises the following question: What are individuals taught in a teacher-education program? While there are some small differences between various colleges and universities, they generally provide similar programs. All schools of education include courses in educational theory. They focus on a variety of popular theories like multiple intelligences, constructivism, behaviourism, brain-based learning and so on. In addition to becoming familiar with these ideas, education students typically learn of their ideal application within the classroom. There is, of course, the practical portion that consists of observing various classrooms and then engaging directly with a classroom of elementary students as a student teacher under the watchful eye of the regular classroom teacher. In some institutions, students may be required to complete an undergraduate course in mathematics before they're accepted into the teacher-education program—typically one that has been designed for education students and covers, in a general way, various math concepts and how they can be taught. The goal of such a math course isn't mastery but exposure.

The primary focus, the very undercurrent of almost every teacher-education program, is self-esteem and social justice.

Standing in the Education Gap

Consider this excerpt from a community newspaper article regarding the local university's teacher-education program:

> "We weave a thread of social justice and reflective practice all the way through the program and apply a lens of social justice to everything that the student teachers observe and learn," Sivia says. "Right from the beginning we disrupt their assumptions about diversity and engage them in a process of reimagining themselves as a socially just teacher through a series of experiences that help them to examine schools and the education system in new ways. The 21st century calls for this kind of teacher."[16]

The entire article highlights various aspects of the university's program and spotlights its focus on training teachers to be "socially just." Nowhere does it describe how they train prospective teachers to be experts, or even proficient, in subject-related skills and knowledge. While we certainly want teachers who are sensitive to the beliefs, backgrounds and lifestyles of their students, teacher-education schools utterly disregard the primary reason for a teacher's existence—to teach subject knowledge—and instead make social justice the centrepiece of their program. In *Ed School Follies*, author Rita Kramer points out this disconnect:

> What matters is not any particular subject or skill, not to preserve past accomplishments or stimulate future achievements, but to give to all that stamp of approval that will make them [students] "feel good about themselves." Self-esteem has replaced understanding as the goal of education.[17]

While I may be belabouring the argument made with regard to the self-esteem movement in the previous chapter, it's important to consider the origin of such attitudes. While many teachers have a positive impact on the lives of their students, are empathetic and are constantly seeking to improve their teaching skills, many are taught in teachers college that the self-esteem of their students comes first.

In addition to the problems discussed earlier, teachers who have learned little more than how to apply teaching theory in a classroom context lack the knowledge to expertly teach young children math, writing and reading. This is of particularly concern when a student advances to the next grade and has huge gaps in her learning. The student not only faces the challenge of being one of many faces in the classroom but also must somehow catch up when the teacher, practically speaking, has neither the luxury of time nor the expertise to help.

The point is not to be critical of individual teachers but of the college programs that train them. The best teachers often disregard much of their teacher training after a few years of working in the classroom since they come to realize that much of what they learned is limited in terms of its practical application. These teachers also look to improve not only on their teaching but also on their mastery of various subjects. While there are, thankfully, many teachers like this, there are simply not enough of them.

Assumption #3
Students Are Taught Essential Learning Skills

Learning skills refer to the routines, habits and attitudes that help students earn and maintain good grades. Study skills, organization, note-taking, initiative and self-monitoring are all examples of learning skills that, as parents, we assume our kids are being taught in school. Unfortunately, apart from helpful hints and reminders from well-meaning teachers, this is often not the case.

While learning skills are one of many areas of importance, I'm often surprised by how seldom teachers and parents make the connection between a lack of organization and poor grades. I have met countless young students who lose assignments, forget due dates, are ill-prepared for tests, take poor notes and constantly lose handouts. Yet these students and their parents wonder what could possibly be going wrong since, after all, they try so hard.

The first mistake we make as parents is in believing that intelligence or hard work alone will produce successful results. Psychologists Joyce Cooper-Kahn and Laurie C. Dietzel, in their book *Late, Lost, and Unprepared*, address the problem with that assumption:

> Many people assume that people with strong intelligence naturally have good executive skills [organizational skills]. We expect "smart" kids to also have strong work habits and the ability to easily manage daily demands at home and school. However, intelligence and executive skills are only moderately correlated.[18]

The sad reality is that even the brightest students can struggle and quickly become discouraged if they haven't mastered and put to consistent use the kind of learning skills that will help them experience better grades.

Our next mistake is assuming that our children will learn these skills in school and, in turn, will be held accountable through consistent monitoring. We make these assumptions because most elementary schools provide planners for their students. Many teachers also write out homework and test due dates on the whiteboard or some other designated place in the classroom. While planners and homework boards are helpful, simply making them available doesn't in any way mean that our schools are teaching kids essential learning skills. While resources are important, ensuring that students actually develop and use learning skills on an ongoing basis requires far more than just helpful hints and occasional reminders. According to Kahn and Dietzel, "we've seen that building better executive functioning occurs over time and most often requires ongoing practice and support."[19]

Assumption #4
Learning Assistance Is Effective for All Struggling Students

The original purpose of a learning resource teacher or department was to provide students with specific academic needs—normally those with a diagnosed learning disability—with one-to-one or small-group learning. Over the years, learning resource teachers' workloads have become inundated with not only students with learning disabilities but also those who have consistent struggles in school not owing to any kind of learning disability. It isn't uncommon for many students to receive a mere 20 to 40 minutes of learning assistance each week, hardly enough to have any meaningful or long-term impact.

While learning assistance is an essential and valuable component of any school, too many parents with children in a learning-assistance program allow themselves to feel a false sense of security. Learning assistance, particularly for those students without a diagnosed learning disability, has little effect on a child's overall academics in the long run if it isn't complemented by the consistent efforts of the parents.

Assumption #5
Students Are Engaged in Learning for the Duration of the School Day

The typical elementary student in North America spends between six and six-and-a-half hours in school. The average day will include subjects like math, language arts, social studies, science and perhaps a foreign language like French or Spanish. Mixed in with these core subjects is a physical-education class and at least one recess or lunch break lasting no less than 30 minutes. When you consider the distractions that naturally take place in a classroom of 20 to 35 students, the window for learning becomes even shorter. So when you break it down, actual teaching and learning take places for about three hours out of every school day.

There are many obvious problems with such a narrow period of time for actual learning to take place. If we focus on just the core subjects of math, reading, writing, social studies and science, it becomes clear that a teacher can't do justice to teaching each of them. Homework is another problem and one, it seems, in which there is no winner. With so little time to cover all the material, it's only natural to assume that there would be more homework. More homework, of course, means less monitoring by the teacher. Yet there are a lot of kids who don't come home with homework, and it makes one wonder how much (or how little) is being covered in the classroom.

The length of the school day is beyond the control of teachers. While it may be tempting to suggest that we should simply increase the length of the school day, there are far too many practical considerations for this to make sense. The problem isn't so much in the number of hours a child spends in school but in the way those hours are utilized. So much of instructional time is spent having students engage in what I would call nonessential activities. Things like group projects and discovery-based exercises tend to take up more time than they deserve, not because they have no place in effective teaching, but because they are used as the primary method of teaching. In addition, with so much focus on ensuring that teaching is student-centred—the teacher serves more as a facilitator and allows the students to dictate the material and pace—relevant and focused instruction rarely takes place.

Assumption #6
Technology Is Widely and Effectively Used

Every so often we read an article in the newspaper or watch a story on television about a school that is utilizing technology by giving laptops or tablet computers to its students. We also learn about things like smartboards—large electronic touchscreens used in place of whiteboards or blackboards. Yet, in practical terms, technology like this is not only rarely utilized, many teachers keep it at arm's length. This doesn't mean that technology can't and won't eventually become an everyday tool in the average classroom—just that, for now, it isn't.

The problem with technology in the classroom isn't the technology itself. It can be an exceptionally useful tool, but it requires a certain level of comfort and familiarity by the classroom teacher as well as formal training in the effective integration and consistent use of computers, tablets and software. A 2008 policy brief from the National Education Association on the subject of technology in schools found that

> Despite the overall progress, many schools are not making full use of technology as a component of comprehensive school reform. The pace of implementation may be slow partly because of competing priorities, and partly because of the lack of reliable information, resources, and expertise on which to make decisions and guide implementation.[20]

There are definitely teachers who put the technology that's available to them—whether computers, smartboards or video projectors—to excellent use. But as a whole, school boards and individual schools put very little planning into precisely how technology is to be used and how teachers are to be formally trained to use it.

Placing technology directly in the hands of students is another gray area. While providing tablet computers for students, as is the case in some schools, sounds like an important step forward, it can be utterly useless unless purposefully integrated with a specific use in mind. Fortunately, there are pilot programs in many schools that are doing exactly that. The flip side is that there are far too many that don't. In reality, laptops or tablet computers, if not used for specific learning tasks, become little more than a novelty. We may hear in the media about how they enhance students' enthusiasm in the classroom, but we rarely hear how, after a few weeks or months, the initial excitement disappears. The devices become more of a distraction and a hindrance than a productive tool.

While a school may have a computer lab and students may engage in a computer class once or twice each week, this doesn't equate to an integration of technology within the everyday classroom setting. In fact, curriculums for the most part don't detail how computers, the Internet or any other sources of technology can be used as tools, particular in the core subjects. Typically, schools and school districts invest hundreds of thousands of dollars in computers, Wi-Fi and so on without any clear guidelines, training or altogether specific purpose.

Assumption #7
Elementary School Adequately Prepares Students for High School and Beyond

Parents typically hold one of two views when it comes to their children's elementary education and its ability to prepare students for high school and, beyond that, college and university. They either feel totally confident that elementary school will adequately prepare their children or feel that elementary school and high school have little connection and that there is virtually no relationship between elementary school and university.

Elementary school should indeed prepare young students for university. I'm not suggesting the type of preparation that involves choosing a university and knowing how to round out a university application. What I mean is that the knowledge, skills, habits and routines students develop in their elementary years can prepare them for university in two different ways.

First, they'll gain the academic skills needed to succeed in high school where, particularly for seniors, grades and experience count toward acceptance into a postsecondary school. Second, skills like organization, prioritizing and studying—as well as persistence, determination and a belief in the inherent value of hard work—are developed in the elementary grades.

Some may assume it's in high school that students acquire the knowledge, skills and attitudes necessary to succeed in university. It's certainly possible for high-school students to learn these things, but the road becomes a much more arduous one after years of lackluster effort. If a student can gain these attributes in elementary school, the path through high school and eventually university becomes a much easier one. Unfortunately, since elementary schools are more concerned with creating children with positive self-esteem, the more challenging but ultimately rewarding lessons and expectations needed to produce a resilient and knowledgeable student are largely ignored.

The importance of our schools can't be overstated. They are, first and foremost, places of learning for our children. We place a lot of faith in their ability to teach our kids, and in doing so we can make the mistake of believing they are fail-safe. Our assumptions about what takes place within the walls of our schools have to be questioned. As parents, we must manage the expectations we have of our schools to teach all that is necessary and valuable to our kids. Our role becomes pivotal since, as we gain a greater appreciation for the strengths and weaknesses of our schools, our understanding of the need to become involved—and how to do so effectively—deepens. Armed with this insight, we can begin to help our children in a practical and confident way.

While I have stated, and will continue to do so, that parents need to be involved in their children's academics, it shouldn't make you feel as though the way forward will be painstaking and time-consuming. Nor do you have to be a trained teacher or an expert in the education of elementary children. What is required is a degree of common sense—something that, as I have pointed out, is often missing in our education system. Common sense, I would argue, is something every well-meaning parent possesses, and if used as a guiding principle, it will make the task of helping your children relatively straightforward. Of course, a little guidance never hurts, and so I'll put a much greater focus on some practical ways parents can help in Section 2 of this book.

CHAPTER 3

The Vagueness of the Curriculum

AS PARENTS WE ASSUME THAT, with each grade, there are a set of specific learning outcomes for each subject area. This, in turn, lays the foundation for the overall curriculum. We also assume that, as children advance from one grade to the next, the learning from the previous year is built upon so that knowledge and experience naturally lead to greater knowledge, more experience and ever-increasing mastery of a particular subject. Unfortunately, this is just not the case. In fact, learning outcomes are seldom specific, and as a result, the curriculum in general is, put simply, vague.

This vagueness in specific learning outcomes is often a cause of much confusion among parents of elementary-school children. Such confusion is all too common when mothers with children in the same grade, but at different schools, compare notes. They quickly discover that one of their kids seems to be much further ahead in reading or math. In fact, as these two moms get deeper in their comparison, the conclusion they may come to is that one of the schools has a higher standard and, therefore, greater expectations of its students.

As parents, a lot of us have probably had experiences that make us wonder why standards and expectations are so very different from one school to another. Not only have I personally come across this phenomenon with my own children, I have also had many conversations with teachers and administrators about this. Perhaps the most telling example occurred when I had the opportunity to visit two separate public schools within the same district on the same day. I had made arrangements to visit with the kindergarten teacher from each school to discuss reading standards.

During my visit to the first school, I met with Ms. Jones (whose name I have changed), the kindergarten teacher. Ms. Jones was a pleasant but no-nonsense teacher. We talked at length about the curriculum and, in particular, her expectations for her kindergarten students once they completed kindergarten. Ms. Jones went through a detailed explanation of how her students were expected to be able to read simple sentences with complete comprehension. She showed me the levelled reading program that she utilized and spoke about decoding strategies, phonetics and expected timelines. In each report card, Ms. Jones was specific about where a particular student was in the reading program, and this formed the basis of her assessment of each child's reading ability. According to Ms. Jones, most of her students left her classroom fully prepared to begin reading basic picture books with simple, age-appropriate sentences.

On that very same day, later in the afternoon, I made my way to the second school to visit Ms. Smith (name also changed). As in my consultation with Ms. Jones only an hour before, we talked about reading standards for kindergarten, and admittedly, I fully expected to receive a very similar response regarding reading readiness as I did from Ms. Jones. What I heard was a stark contrast. Ms. Smith explained to me that the general purpose of the curriculum in kindergarten was to prepare children for academic life in Grade 1 and beyond. This preparation had little, if anything, to do with academic preparation. It was about laying the groundwork for children to thrive in an environment with other children from different backgrounds and with different ideas, beliefs and interests. This was accomplished through the teaching of manners, social skills and an attitude of inclusion. When I pressed further and asked about specific objectives for reading, Ms. Smith made it clear that kindergarten was too young an age to expect children to read much beyond simple, single-syllable words. The reading, she explained, would come naturally as they progressed through Grade 1 and beyond.

How is it possible to have two vastly different standards and expectations for kindergarten reading within the same school district? The answer can be found in the prescribed learning outcomes laid out by the province of British Columbia. For example, here are three prescribed learning outcomes outlined by the BC Ministry of Education regarding reading in kindergarten:

It is expected that students will:
B1 Demonstrate awareness of the connection between reading, writing and oral language

B2 Respond to literature through a variety of activities (e.g., role playing, art, music, choral reading, talking)

B3 Engage in reading or reading-like behaviour[21]

These prescribed learning outcomes (PLOs) include suggested achievement indicators like "understand that we can read 'talk' that has been written down," "locate a specific (generally familiar) word," "show enthusiasm for, or enjoyment of, reading (e.g. choose and read and/or view a variety of texts that interest them)" and "self-select texts on the basis of interest or familiarity."

Of course, there are more PLOs and a variety of other suggested achievement indicators, but I have chosen these few by way of example. When we examine these PLOs, it's clear that they are not only vague but also open to interpretation. Even the achievement indicators are mere suggestions and hardly specific. How does a child adequately demonstrate that she understands we can read "talk" that has been written down? How does a child sufficiently demonstrate an enthusiasm for reading?

In Ms. Jones's opinion, these PLOs mean that once a child completes kindergarten, he or she should be able to read simple sentences. For Ms. Smith, they mean that her job as the teacher is to develop an early love for learning and a spirit of cooperation and to nurture the anticipation of reading enjoyment that will come in the following grades.

Which teacher is on the right path? Since the curriculum and PLOs are so hazy, how can we challenge either teacher's interpretation? You would likely find that, if you pose these questions to a handful of parents, they would be divided. Some parents feel that kindergarten, being a child's first real classroom experience, should be devoid of the pressures that come with academic achievement. Others would say that the sooner a child begins to master the basics of reading or math, the greater the chance of academic success in the future.

When we don't have specific learning outcomes with specific achievement indicators, we leave our children open to any number of gaps in their learning. Ms. Smith assumes that the basic elements of reading will come eventually, perhaps in Grade 1, perhaps later. If the curriculum doesn't specify precisely what a student should learn, then how, as parents, can we have faith that essential skills will be taught by the next teacher?

Standing in the Education Gap

What Is Going On?

If it makes complete sense to have specific and clear learning objectives for each grade, then why is the curriculum in provinces and states across North America so vague? Let's look at some of the concerns and questionable beliefs that lead educators to keep the curriculum loose and flexible.

Controversy Over What Is Important to Learn and When

When you begin to wade through all of the varying opinions on what elementary students should learn, at what point in their development, and in what manner, it becomes quite clear that there isn't a lot of agreement. It's not hard to see that governments and district administrators are stuck between a rock and a hard place. Choose specific content and resources with which the content is to be taught and you risk attracting criticism from those who feel this kind of rigid approach stifles discovery, creativity and self-esteem. Go in the opposite direction, and others will voice their concerns over the lack of specific content. The solution? Leave just enough room for interpretation to satisfy all parties. Provide wording that allows for enough wiggle room for schools and teachers to manoeuvre while, at the same time, maintaining some semblance of uniformity.

Discovery More Important Than Mastery

The elementary-school curriculum favours a discovery approach to learning. In a nutshell, when young students are allowed to discover knowledge for themselves, information naturally becomes more meaningful. Greater meaning leads to a higher form of thinking that in turn leads to a love of learning. Direct instruction, memorization and constant practice and drills, we are told, will only kill a child's love for learning and, ultimately, her self-esteem. According to this theory, the curriculum must allow teachers to construct a classroom environment and a method of teaching that helps a child discover not only knowledge but also the means by which she learns best.

Emphasis on Interests, Abilities and Areas of Intelligence

If the curriculum and learning outcomes were specific with regard to the content a child was to learn, the resources to be utilized and the way in which progress was to be assessed, we would be discriminating against countless students. How so? We would be completely disregarding the variety of abilities, interests and "areas" of intelligence to be found in the average classroom. A vague curriculum ensures that each child is given a fair chance to demonstrate her abilities without having to conform to an approach or a method of assessment that doesn't complement her particular way of learning. For example, instead of a research paper on the Renaissance, a middle-school student could choose to create an album cover depicting important elements of the Renaissance, make a diorama or compose song lyrics.

Knowledge and Information Are Constantly Changing

Changes in technology continually influence the way we understand things, the way we organize and use information, and the way we work. Since our ultimate goal is to prepare our children for life after school and in the workplace, what and how we teach must also reflect changes in information and technology. If the curriculum and its learning outcomes were rigid, static and clearly defined, we would risk leaving students unprepared for what lies ahead. The curriculum shouldn't be seen as vague but as flexible and open, allowing for teachers to meet the ever-changing demands of a constantly evolving world.

The Fallout

While there are educators who would decry such an observation, the reality is that a vague curriculum is a serious problem. It has a definite and negative impact on how our kids learn and what they learn.

Wasted Time

Each September, without fail, teachers in classrooms across North America spend the first several weeks of the school year reviewing material from the prior grade. Reviewing material from the previous year, particularly after a long summer holiday, isn't unproductive. However, since there is no common and specific knowledge and skill-set laid out in the elementary curriculum, the classroom will be filled with students of varying levels of understanding and experience. When a student begins a new year in a new grade with a new teacher, she may need more than just review—she may have wide gaps in her learning.

Now, instead of reviewing common curriculum material from the previous year, classroom teachers must spend inordinate amounts of time reviewing or even teaching material that should have been sufficiently covered in the previous grade. In addition, while it's expected that students in a classroom will require occasional one-to-one attention from the teacher, many elementary school teachers end up spending much of their time moving from one child to the next instead of teaching the class as a whole. As a result, students become bored, since they either must wait to be taught the material in order to move forward or are completely familiar with the information being reviewed and must wait for their struggling classmates to catch up before learning anything new.

Growing Achievement Gaps Between Students

One of the greatest challenges for elementary teachers is to somehow make lessons meaningful, memorable and lasting for a classroom of students of varying academic abilities. When PLOs are vague they create a gap between students within the same grade. For example, those students who engage in more writing-centred projects typically become more advanced in their writing skills than those who constantly create posters, dioramas, slide shows, album covers and so forth. It's common sense to assume that, the more a child writes (paying attention to grammar and punctuation, among other things), the more proficient she will become at writing. Now, observe a large classroom of middle-school students. There will be a noticeable lag in the writing skills of many of these students. This achievement gap only increases with each passing grade as teachers struggle to progress through the year and meet the needs of the variety of students within the classroom.

Students Are Ill-Prepared for Postsecondary Education

While I've already alluded to how our education system doesn't adequately prepare students for college, it bears repeating. To the shock and dismay of many first-year university students, the standards and expectations in your typical university are a world apart from what they experienced in high school. Unlike elementary and secondary schools, universities expect students to come prepared with certain academic skills, whether it's a proficiency in math and the sciences or a mastery of essay writing, including the use of proper grammar and punctuation. Since the elementary curriculum doesn't define specific skills that build upon each other with each successive grade, students carry the gaps in their knowledge through high school, and after that, graduating students find themselves completely unprepared for the academic rigours of university.

Repetition of Material

The following is a comparison of the PLOs for Language Arts between Grade 3, 4, 5, 6 and 7 in the province of British Columbia.

Grade 3:
C1 Create a variety of clear personal writing and representations that express connections to personal experiences, ideas, and opinions, featuring
- ideas supported by related details
- sentence fluency using a variety of sentence lengths and patterns
- experimentation with word choice by using new and different words
- an emerging voice demonstrating a developing writing style
- an organization that is meaningful and logical

Grade 4:
C1 Write clear, focussed personal writing for a range of purposes and audiences that demonstrates

connections to personal experiences, ideas, and opinions, featuring
- clearly developed ideas using effective supporting details and explanations
- sentence fluency through a variety of sentence lengths and patterns, with some emerging fluidity
- experimentation with word choice by using new, different, more precise and powerful words
- an authentic voice demonstrating a developing writing style
- an organization that is meaningful, logical, and effective, and showcases a central idea or theme

Grade 5:

C1 Write a variety of clear, focussed personal writing for a range of purposes and audiences that demonstrates connections to personal experiences, ideas, and opinions, featuring
- clearly developed ideas by using effective supporting details, explanations, and comparisons
- sentence fluency through sentence variety and lengths, with increasing rhythm and flow
- effective word choice by using a greater number of new, powerful, and more precise words
- an emerging and honest voice
- an organization that is meaningful, logical, and effective, and showcases a central idea or theme

Grade 6:

C1 Write a variety of clear, focussed personal writing for a range of purposes and audiences that demonstrates connections to personal experiences, ideas, and opinions, featuring
- clearly developed ideas by using effective supporting details, explanations, comparisons, and insights
- sentence fluency through sentence variety and lengths with increasing rhythm and flow
- effective word choice through the use of an increasing number of new, varied, and powerful words
- an honest voice
- an organization that is meaningful, logical, and effective, and showcases a central idea or theme

Grade 7:

C1 Write a variety of clear, focussed personal writing for a range of purposes and audiences that demonstrates connections to personal experiences, ideas, and opinions, featuring
- clearly developed ideas by using effective supporting details, explanations, analysis, and insights
- sentence fluency through sentence variety and patterns with increasingly natural rhythm and flow
- effective word choice through the use of precise nouns, and powerful verbs and modifiers
- an honest and engaging voice
- an organization that is meaningful, logical, and effective, and showcases a central idea or theme[22]

As you can see, from Grade 3 through Grade 7—five years—the PLOs are, in almost every case, identical. There are minor additions in some years, but on the whole, one would have trouble identifying one grade from the next. In addition, if we set aside the clear repetition of outcomes, there is virtually no detail or specificity as to what knowledge a student in any of these grades should acquire and master. The result? Information and skills tend to be repeated, not built upon, from one grade to the next.

No Clear Assessment of Skills or Knowledge Acquisition

Most provinces and states do include suggested achievement indicators. These suggested achievement indicators are typically generic and broad, allowing great flexibility for teachers to assess a student's learning in any way they see fit. It's important to point out that teachers should be given some freedom with regard to how they grade their students and what forms of evaluation and assessment they will use. However, the problem that typically occurs is in the difference in standards between one teacher and another in a similar grade.

Without specific achievement indicators, the standards of one teacher may greatly differ from that of another. I have worked with a number of teachers who applied all sorts of different criteria for handing out grades. Years ago, one colleague shared with me that no student in her class could earn an A unless he or she demonstrated writing skills beyond grade level. When I asked what, in her opinion, were the achievement standards that determined if a student had skills "beyond" grade level, her response was that she simply had enough experience to be able to tell. How could I argue, since there were no clear and specific learning outcomes for her to follow? While she was certainly an experienced teacher, in reality her criteria were based on a comparison of her students and not on a clearly defined achievement standard that was measurable and objective.

On the other end of the spectrum, I have conversed with many teachers who base their grading criteria, at least in part, on a student's effort. In extreme cases I have encountered those who have withheld a high grade not because a student didn't demonstrate a full understanding of the material, but because that student didn't put enough effort into her work to reach her full potential. Is any of this fair? Absolutely not. Is it reality? Absolutely.

Knowledge Built Upon Knowledge

When you have vague, generic and repetitive learning outcomes, you open the door for too much flexibility and interpretation. Common sense tells us that the curriculum should be specific in its content, specific about which grade content must be taught and learned, and specific with regard to how schools should assess whether or not students have actually learned the content. There should be no overlap from grade to grade, but instead there should be a progression of subject matter from one grade to the next. In other words, building knowledge upon knowledge.

Does this mean that teachers should be given no flexibility in the way they teach? No, but nor should we allow classrooms to be student-centred environments where the material taught is dictated, in large part, by the interests of the students. Teachers should have the flexibility to utilize a variety of tools at their disposal to teach a common curriculum to classrooms full of children with various interests and backgrounds. I emphasize tools because, too often, approaches and methodologies that can supplement and complement tried and true techniques become the ends, not the means, by which teachers teach.

Unfortunately, common sense in education is not always common. Even when curriculum reforms are mandated, very little actually changes. As parents, we can ensure that our children acquire the knowledge they need and help them build upon that knowledge year after year. Our efforts at home can not only complement the efforts of our schools but also greatly enhance our children's learning. The good news is that all that is required of us, as parents, is consistency—not knowledge of teaching methodology or experience in a classroom setting, just our regular attention. If we are purposeful and consistent, our time and effort will feel surprisingly light, not because it's altogether easy, but because all that is required are small but significant changes. More on that later.

Chapter 4

Learning Through Discovery

THE NUMBER-ONE GOAL OF THE elementary classroom is to produce students who have "higher-order thinking skills." Higher-order thinking, briefly, involves skills that allow a student to independently observe new information or unfamiliar problems, come to an understanding as to how something works and, if applicable, find a correct solution. Imagine your child with the ability to successfully solve a variety of academic challenges through careful observation, critical thinking and, ultimately, discovery. It wouldn't be hard to imagine that, if a young student could gain an understanding of math through problem-solving, grasp the significance of history, appreciate world issues or write with creativity and technical accuracy, then learning would become highly enjoyable and motivating. The more a child can enjoy learning, the more meaningful and memorable lessons become. However, it isn't the goals that are being called into question, it's the way in which our education system believes they can be achieved that is so dubious. As we'll find out, in our attempts to help students learn and nurture higher-order thinking skills, our schools have turned their backs on common sense.

Marc Lapointe

The Philosophy of Discovery Learning

How, then, do our schools propose to develop higher-order thinking skills in their students? For the most part, it's through a philosophy of teaching known as "discovery learning." It's also known by many other names, such as "constructivism," "inquiry-based learning," "child-centred learning," "hands-on learning," "project-based learning", "collaborative learning" and "self-directed learning". In short, discovery learning views students as active learners. Meaningful learning takes place in an environment where students are challenged to discover solutions to problems without the direct instruction of the classroom teacher. An "active" classroom would consist of a number of components, such as having the students sit in grouped desks, assigning numerous projects and working through countless word problems. If you were to enter into this kind of classroom environment, it would definitely have the appearance of activity.

Exploration and problem-solving are at the heart of the discovery approach. A classroom teacher's job is to create activities that encourage the integration of new knowledge with the student's current knowledge base. This way, learning becomes meaningful and more memorable, since students should be making relevant connections on their own, without direct instruction or intervention by the teacher.

Discovery learning places an emphasis on the individual interests and learning styles of each student. The teacher, therefore, takes on the role of facilitator. According to advocates of discovery learning, this approach is different from a teacher-centred classroom environment where students typically take on a more passive role. Traditionally, this involves the teacher lecturing or doing demonstrations and examples while the students sit and watch.

Standing in the Education Gap

Very few parents can deny that a philosophy of education that seeks to put the needs of the individual child first sounds nothing but positive. After all, don't many of us learn well by doing something instead of reading about it? Isn't the ultimate goal for our kids to love the learning process, since with such an attitude, academic success can't be far behind? Yet, particularly in subjects like math and writing, students are struggling more and more with basic, foundational concepts.

Take math as an example. In most elementary classrooms across North America, math textbooks contain very little by way of lesson, example and practice. Instead, they are chock-full of word problems designed to stimulate a greater degree of critical thought. Word problems by themselves are not the issue; it's the lack of clear instruction and examples that have so many parents in fits. The idea, of course, is that different kids learn to find the right answers to math problems using different strategies. The teacher, instead of telling students the procedures necessary to find the answer, must serve as a facilitator whose purpose is to ensure that students have a general understanding of the concepts. The assumption is that if a student can grasp a new concept, procedure will naturally follow.

Unfortunately, this is often the exact opposite of what happens. Without a thorough foundation in basic skills or procedures, a general concept may be vaguely understood, but the student will rarely come to the right answer. How can we expect a child to wrestle through a word problem where, in order to come up with the correct answer, subtracting two or three digit numbers is involved, but the student has not yet mastered subtraction? More often than not, in order to overcome this obstacle, students are allowed, even encouraged, to use calculators to complete basic computations. After all, procedure only gets in the way of understanding the concepts.

We can see the discovery approach to learning in subjects outside of math as well. In language arts, for example, there is more focus on ensuring that students engage in assignments that meet their interests than in teaching and practicing essential skills in writing. Instead of giving writing assignments for evaluation, elementary students are given the freedom to draw, create a video or slide show, build a model or engage in any number of activities that the student may be more interested in. Projects like these are considered far more engaging than a writing assignment. The result? Essential writing skills are lacking.

Where Has All the Common Sense Gone? The Realities of Discovery Learning

Richard E. Clark, Paul A. Kirschner and John Sweller make the following statement in an article in the journal *American Educator*, "Putting Students on the Path to Learning: The Case for Fully Guided Instruction":

> Decades of research clearly demonstrate that *for novices* (comprising virtually all students), direct, explicit instruction is more effective and more efficient than partial guidance. So, when teaching new content and skills to novices, teachers are more effective when they provide explicit guidance accompanied by practice and feedback, not when they require students to discover many aspects of what they must learn.[23]

Time and again, it has been demonstrated that discovery learning, particularly when intended to teach new skills and information, rarely results in effective and meaningful learning for the student. As our system of education continues to forge ahead in either complete ignorance of this fact or with stubborn determination, it's the education of our children that suffers.

Wasted Time

Discovery learning takes a lot of time. In fact, it's rare for elementary teachers to get through the entire curriculum over the course of the school year, in large part because so much time is spent trying to facilitate a student's learning through discovery. When you consider all of the variables involved in teaching a classroom of 20 to 35 students, the amount of time spent attempting to help so many kids engage in some form of discovery increases exponentially.

If we were to examine discovery learning strictly within the context of a return on time invested, we would come to the conclusion that, for the most part, it's time that isn't spent wisely. In his book *The Schools We Need and Why We Don't Have Them*, author E. D. Hirsch, Jr., addresses this:

> It is true, on the other hand, that self-generated student-constructed learning (discovery learning) is sometimes better retained and more readily accessible than constructed learning that is teacher-induced. But if discovery learning is well retained, it also has drawbacks. It takes more time and is sometimes insecure in its results—insecure not in the durability of what is remembered but in the content of what is remembered. Students "discover" all sorts of things, some of them irrelevant to the purposes at hand and some of them wrong.[24]

A discovery approach to learning does have a place. But discovery—particularly in the elementary grades—is, at best, a risky proposition when we neglect to directly teach foundational procedures first. When you consider not only the time but also the uncertainty of the outcome, "investment" is perhaps not the best word to use when discussing discovery learning. We should instead compare it to high-stakes gambling. Relying on students to discover the correct procedures, concepts and solutions in any subject area is a perilous endeavour.

Inundated With Projects

One of the most popular methods to promote discovery in the classroom is through the use of projects—dioramas, posters, slide shows, cover art, models, lyrics and so on. The problem is not that projects aren't engaging and therefore useful, but that they're the means by which students discover new information. In the words of Clark, Kirschner and Weller, "small group and independent problems and projects can be effective—not as vehicles for making discoveries, but as a means of *practicing* recently learned content and skills."[25]

Whenever teachers rely on projects as a means by which students acquire knowledge and skills, mastery and application are almost completely neglected. Assessments also become fuzzy and, not surprisingly, subjective. Let's take a look at the go-to project of the elementary classroom: the diorama. Students are required to create a scene or model of an event or place. The goal of the diorama is to give students the opportunity to show creativity and to find out all they can about a particular topic in the process. The information a student acquires must be reflected in the model. The assessment becomes a sliding scale. Different students may "discover" different things; models will reflect varying degrees of thought and creativity, and inevitably, many of the students' parents will play a significant role in the creation of the model. Is it fair to grade a student who has created a model from start to finish completely on her own without any help from her parents more harshly than a diorama that is simply stellar but was clearly put together by the parents?

Some teachers, in an effort to avoid unfair parental involvement, dedicate class time to project work. While this may solve one problem, it doesn't address the issue of what knowledge is necessary for a student to acquire. On top of that, as we've already found out, a classroom full of busy students may look productive but time is often wasted—especially when you consider what that time could have been used for.

Compounding Academic Problems

If the goal of elementary education is to help students discover solutions and meanings, how are we to accurately pinpoint specific gaps in their learning? If, for example, a student in Grade 4 or 5 can't successfully answer a question involving long division, and our primary concern is conceptual understanding, what do we say is the problem? Is it fair for a teacher to suggest that the student isn't working hard enough or paying enough attention in class? If the teacher is merely a facilitator, then there is very little, if any, direct instruction for a child to pay attention to. We can't fault a student's effort since she may feel she has discovered all that is important or necessary. The questions and problems continue to build on each other with no clear answers in sight.

Having clear guidelines as to the specific knowledge a student must master allows teachers and parents to identify academic problems and, in turn, give workable solutions on how a child may be helped. Let's go back to the example of the student who has trouble with long division. I've observed that, among other things, students who can't complete a long-division problem correctly are often unable to subtract properly. If a child can't perform the foundational procedure of subtracting numbers without the use of a calculator, then it should come as no surprise that she struggles with more complex math problems. The best way to begin helping a student like this is to teach her how to subtract and then have her practice until it is relatively easy. Without direct instruction of these procedures, children will continue to struggle in math with each succeeding grade. We will deal more directly with these issues in a more practical way in Section 2.

Throwing the Baby Out With the Bathwater

Direct instruction, memorization and practice are deeply frowned upon by advocates of discovery learning. At best, these are perceived as "old school" teaching practices, but more often they are vilified as completely choking out fun and meaning from learning. What could be more boring and unmotivating than asking children to memorize their times table or to sit at their desks listening to a teacher lecture through math class or language arts? The discovery approach seeks to do away with these supposed enemies of meaningful learning in the hope of producing students who not only learn more effectively but also develop a love for learning that lasts a lifetime.

I've already alluded to the fact that, in proper context, projects, problem-solving and group collaboration can have a lot of value in the classroom. Yet advocates of the discovery approach completely reject any "traditional" teaching methods—even if they have proven to be useful, if not superior, in helping students learn necessary skills. Unfortunately, our elementary schools, for the most part, choose to ignore these facts and instead continue the practice of guiding students without ensuring that they have the tools necessary for understanding and, later, critical thought.

Passing the Buck

Back in Chapter 1 I told a story about a disturbing trend I encountered in my early years as a teacher, particularly as I first began my career. As you may recall, I wrote about how students were entering my math class with numerous gaps in their understanding. I had assumed that, by Grade 8, every student should be able to successfully complete a long-division question, multiply three or four digit numbers or, at the very least, subtract three or four lines of large numbers. Nothing could be further from the truth. I often found that at least half of my students instinctively reached for their calculators even when adding single-digit numbers. What I discovered, besides the fact that some of my colleagues were allowing their students to have easy access to calculators, was that there was a great disparity between what and how other teachers taught. These differences were not only, at times, contrary to my own expectations, but often there were marked differences – and conflicting expectations – between many of the teachers.

I also found out that some of these teachers assumed that, if a child hadn't quite mastered subtraction or multiplication (even though it should have been expected that they would), she would eventually learn it from her parents or in the next grade. Of course, this rarely was the case, since parents weren't made aware of the problem, or their child's lack of basic knowledge wasn't deemed a problem by the teacher, or the parents made the same mistake as their child's teacher and assumed it would be taught the following year. Not only were these assumptions way off the mark, they contributed to a snowball effect where gaps continued to pile up with each successive grade. Meanwhile, parents develop a sense of false security, believing that no news is good news.

Marc Lapointe

If There Are So Many Problems With Discovery Learning, Why Do it?

Let's examine the most common arguments for the exclusive use of discovery learning in our elementary classrooms.

We Haven't Pursued It to Its Full Potential

From the perspective of discovery-learning proponents, teachers are simply not following the approach rigorously enough. In other words, if one doesn't strictly adhere to the methods espoused by the discovery-based approach, then one can't expect to observe its full potential. The response by our system of education, therefore, is to push more and more toward the "ideal" discovery-based program, regardless of the obvious fact that our students fall further and further behind in essential math and writing skills.

The argument that our system of education has not immersed itself enough in discovery-based learning is a weak one. Teacher-education programs across Canada and the United States are saturated with these concepts. Not a single teacher graduates from a teacher-education program without being armed with the purpose of helping students "learn how to learn." While the notion of child-centred learning has been a part of teacher-education programs for decades, one need only peer back four decades to a teacher-education textbook on elementary education to see that this idea is neither new nor inadequately pursued in our system of education. The 1976 textbook *Teaching and Learning in the Elementary School* describes a process by which "children are encouraged to find things out for themselves by applying the scientific method of inquiry. Through inquiry, they should learn how to learn. Inquiry stresses discovering things for oneself."[26]

Even the textbooks our children use, particularly math texts, have been developed with an emphasis on discovery for years. They emphasize open-ended problem-solving, dialoguing and conceptual understanding. All of this sounds great, but it lacks sound judgment. This approach to teaching math is, at heart, a discovery-based approach that focuses not on teaching foundational, procedural skills but on allowing students to discern learning through higher-order reasoning. Regardless of what one may feel about this kind of math program, it's nothing new.

It Is the Best Approach in a World of Ever-Changing Knowledge and Information

Another argument in support of the discovery method is that it's the best way for students to "learn how to learn." In other words, if a child can ultimately learn new concepts through methods that are best suited to her interests and style of learning then meaningful, authentic and lasting learning has taken place. In a world full of knowledge and information that is changing and increasing at a blistering pace, students must be taught how to adapt to constant changes. In order to ensure that students are prepared and can keep up, our goal must be to teach them how to learn.

It only makes sense that the ability to adapt to changing information and ever-increasing knowledge requires that young students have a solid foundation in concepts that don't change. Yet what makes sense doesn't always apply to our elementary schools. The rules of math are constant, even though as parents we sometimes find ourselves believing that they have changed or evolved since we were kids. The skills needed for reading and writing have always been the same regardless of the many approaches used to teach those skills. We can't expect that students will somehow "learn how to learn" without some form of direct instruction that lays the foundation for the knowledge and skills that eventually lead to this higher educational ideal.

Marc Lapointe

It Promotes Higher-Order Thinking Skills

This is one of the most commonly heard "buzz" phrases in elementary education. As mentioned earlier, higher-order thinking skills are those abilities that allows individuals to successfully navigate through challenging and complex problems or to make connections from information and, in turn, uncover deeper meanings or reveal possible solutions. In the elementary grades, the ultimate goal is for young students to make correct connections on their own, whether through problem-solving in math or scrutinizing a certain text. Higher-order thinking skills allow a child to naturally discover the answers.

To help students achieve this valuable skill, our elementary-education system promotes a number of approaches. In math, we have steered away from procedural knowledge—in other words, the mechanics of basic math like subtraction, addition, multiplication and division—in favour of a conceptual knowledge. The idea is that, if a child can be made to understand the idea behind a particular math concept, the mechanics will eventually and naturally follow. The most popular elementary math texts are chock-full of word problems; instead of direct instruction and example, they attempt to subtly lead the student toward understanding through discovery-based questions and observations.

When it comes to writing, the same general idea applies. Rarely are young students taught the mechanics of writing, such as grammar, punctuation and spelling. Instead they are encouraged to engage in free writing. The purpose of free writing is to ensure that writing is less about being technically correct and more about being creative. If a child doesn't have to focus on proper grammar or spelling, writing becomes a more enjoyable and meaningful process. Once that's been achieved, the technical aspect of writing will naturally follow.

Higher-order thinking is a valuable goal. To have the ability to draw meaning from complex problems can only be of great benefit to our students. However, in the average elementary classroom, the "goal" becomes the means instead of the eventual and successful end point. Does it make sense to expect a young student to think critically about subject matter without having first mastered the procedures or attained the requisite knowledge? You wouldn't allow your child to take the wheel of the family car if she had never driven before—even though she may have had years sitting in the back seat, casually watching you drive. She may understand the concept of driving, but without knowing the procedures—everything from the mechanics of putting the car in gear and manoeuvring through traffic to the laws of the road—we would never think of allowing her to simply drive away. Yet we seem to have few issues with allowing our children to advance through math barely able to add or subtract or without the ability to multiply or work through long-division problems. We accept writing that is disorganized and technically sloppy in favour of the creative process.

We Should Encourage What Makes Each Child Unique

A discovery-based approach allows children to emphasize their uniqueness. After all, if every child were taught in the same manner, with the same procedures and using the same content, there would be nothing special about each child. We are a society that is careful to recognize what makes an individual child special, even in the most mundane accomplishments. If we fail to do so, we threaten our children's sense of self-worth and self-esteem.

Once again, this argument fails to consider that, in order for students to discover their own unique interests and talents, they must first learn the core skills. A young student may never realize her creative gifts, for example, if we don't teach her the fundamentals of writing. With these essential skills in place, she is equipped to share her talent for creative storytelling. By not helping students master essential skills in writing, reading or math, we are, in fact, contributing to a child's *lack* of confidence and self-worth.

Few people realize, or they fail to consider, that the father of Amadeus Mozart was, in fact, a musician and teacher. It's common for many of us, when we think of the musical genius of Mozart, to assume he was somehow born with the ability to fully compose remarkable concertos. Yet it was Mozart's father who took the time to teach his son music from a very young age, starting him along his amazing path. I'm not suggesting that Mozart didn't have musical talent—even exceptional talent—to begin with. However, his father didn't merely sit back to see what would develop. He taught his son, directly, all of the basic skills needed to not only uncover prodigious ability but also excel with it. While our children may not demonstrate the giant talents of someone like Mozart, the message is clear: The mastery of basic, fundamental skills is the key to uncovering the interests and abilities of our kids.

"Traditional" Teaching Is Boring

The term "drill and kill" is well known among teachers and educators. It refers to the use of repetitive drills in order to memorize and, ultimately, master basic skills. "Drill and kill" carries the implication that anything involving repetition, memorization or moderate amounts of practice is not only the wrong way to teach but can ultimately destroy a child's willingness to learn. Since this is the dominant philosophy in our schools, anything that is not deemed as nurturing a love for learning or self-esteem is considered inferior and unwelcome. In an effort to counter the perceived shortcomings of the so-called "drill and kill" approach, our education system has followed the concept of project-based teaching.

Earlier, we examined the use of projects for learning. Besides being a platform for "discovery," they have also been a reaction to so-called "drill and kill" methods and seek to accomplish several goals:

- To make learning more hands-on and therefore meaningful;

- To step away from the traditional, more isolated focus on subjects like language arts or social studies and create connections between disciplines; and

- To allow children to demonstrate what they have learned through a medium that best suits their individual learning styles.

As one of many teaching tools available to a classroom teacher, creative projects can be extremely useful and refreshing for both the students and the teacher. However, as is often the case in the world of elementary education, seldom is a practical balance achieved. Within many classrooms, the project-based method is almost exclusively used for teaching and assessment. The problem? Large gaps in student learning inevitably follow.

I have personally witnessed the pitfalls of strictly adhering to a project-based approach to teaching. In a particular Grade 6 class, students were required to engage in "reading responses." In other words, with every book that they read, they were required to reflect on the story through any number of short projects. Their options ranged from the creation of movie posters, album covers and song lyrics to short skits or slide presentations. An actual written response was last on the list. In addition, students could choose to read from magazines, comics, novels or books containing diagrams.

At first glance, this approach to reading responses appears to be a generally positive one. It allows students to be creative, show off their interests and talents and, hopefully, become motivated to read. From this perspective, the project-based approach does have many merits. There are, however, several problems associated with these kinds of assignments. First, in this particular circumstance, the only requirements were that students make a choice as to which type of response they would utilize. They could choose the same project each time, meaning that, if a child wished to create a movie poster for each book or comic book she had finished, that was okay. Second, at no time were these various assignment choices designed to reinforce essential reading and writing skills. Third, grading of the projects was unequal. A child who spent very little time or effort on an album cover could conceivably receive the same grade as a child who worked tirelessly on a written response. Finally, since even comic books were considered acceptable, many students were by no means challenged or intellectually stimulated.

This example is typical of learning in the elementary classroom today. In many classrooms, students are constantly involved in some project or another, either individually or with a group. Our desire to motivate students to learn, to discover and to engage academically, while well-intentioned, doesn't address the need to acquire knowledge and skills and then, with each succeeding grade, build upon that knowledge and those skills. Giving elementary students choice in many aspects of their learning, particularly through endless projects, is not teaching but merely keeping them busy.

Standing in the Education Gap

A Balanced Approach

Clark, Kirschner and Sweller observed the following:

> Many educators (especially teacher education professors in colleges of education) have latched on to this notion of students having to "construct" their own knowledge, and have *assumed* that the best way to promote such construction is to have students try to discover new knowledge or solve new problems without explicit guidance from the teacher. Unfortunately, this assumption is both widespread and incorrect.[27]

While I have written at some length about the many pitfalls of discovery-based learning and project-based teaching, I do believe that these methods have a valuable place within the classroom. They are, as I've suggested, tools available to the classroom teacher. The problem is that, in our current system of elementary education, these approaches aren't viewed as merely tools but as the foundation on which we should teach. As Clark, Kirschner and Sweller have aptly alluded to, it's unreasonable to expect that young students will somehow discover—and discover correctly—new knowledge without direct teaching.

Of course, not every school pays strict adherence to the idea of discovery-based learning, and many have begun to see how unreasonable a system without explicit and direct teaching really is. But the unhindered belief that, through pure discovery, our children will receive the best education is deeply engrained in the minds of many of our teachers and educational professionals, starting with teacher-education programs. Any shift in this philosophy will take years, and our students can't afford to wait until this shift happens—if ever it does. That's why I am constantly encouraging parents to take action on behalf of their children. All that is required on our part, as parents, are small but regular and effective changes in how we help our kids outside of the classroom. Once we get to Section 2, you'll see exactly what kinds of small changes I'm talking about.

CHAPTER 5

Individual Learning Styles

AS PARENTS, WE RECOGNIZE THAT our children have certain interests, routines and ways of learning new skills and remembering new information. It's also obvious that children (or adults for that matter) aren't all the same when it comes to interests and learning preferences. Since this is the case, it would seem to make sense that, as we attempt to teach a child something new and complex, we do our best to find a method of teaching that will help that particular child learn effectively and quickly.

In general, this is the challenge that our elementary schools continually wrestle with. How, in a classroom full of children, can we ensure that we're meeting the individual needs of each child? In order to answer this question, educators refer to something called "individual learning styles." It's a theory that proposes that every student has a particular way in which she learns best. This idea has been around for some time but has been popularized in the last two decades. For many teachers, especially those fresh out of teachers' college, it is one of the guiding principles of effective classroom teaching.

Marc Lapointe

Multiple Intelligences

In order to understand what individual learning styles are and how the idea was popularized, it's helpful to take a closer look at the very theory that gave it life—the Theory of Multiple Intelligences (MI). First proposed by a Harvard professor named Howard Gardner in 1983, MI suggests that intelligence can't be defined by a narrow construct like IQ. Instead, MI proposes seven distinct intelligences.

- *Linguistic Intelligence*: This area of intelligence is used for things like reading, writing and comprehension of the spoken and written word.

- *Logical-Mathematical Intelligence*: Those who have the ability to solve mathematical problems or use logic and deduction are said to possess this type of intelligence.

- *Spatial Intelligence*: If you can get from one place to another by reading a map or efficiently pack items into a box, then you have spatial intelligence.

- *Musical Intelligence*: As the term suggests, people with musical intelligence can appreciate a piece of music, read and write music, play an instrument or sing along to a song.

- *Bodily-Kinaesthetic Intelligence*: This domain involves overall athletic ability, whether it's hitting a baseball, shooting a puck, running, dancing or other endeavours.

- *Interpersonal Intelligence*: Those with interpersonal

intelligence have the ability to relate to other people and can seemingly understand a person's emotions and behaviour.

- *Intrapersonal Intelligence*: This is best described as being able to understand oneself or, in other words, having a distinct awareness of one's own abilities and beliefs: generally, what makes oneself tick.

Many of us could probably claim to have some level of "intelligence" in each of these domains. However, according to Gardner, an individual will typically show a much a higher level of intelligence in one of these domains as compared to all of the others.

Multiple Intelligences in the Classroom

Having a general idea with regard to what MI actually is, the next question might be what its relevance is to the average elementary classroom in North America. Quite simply, if we were to hold to the notion that each child shows an aptitude in one of the domains, then it would make sense for teachers to teach according to an individual child's particular area of intelligence. This notion has further evolved into the idea of individual learning styles. This theory assumes that one individual student doesn't learn the same way as another student. The reason? Each student displays a different intelligence and, therefore, requires a different approach.

Proponents of individual learning styles point out that part of the reason some children struggle in school is because a one-size-fits-all approach to teaching only serves to decrease motivation and overall achievement. How can we expect each child to benefit from memorizing her times tables when, perhaps, her learning style is much more "tactile" or "visual"? Instead, a teacher should present information in a way that matches the child's specific learning style.

Practically speaking, it's apparent that attempting to teach in a way that meets each child's learning style can be a massive challenge. The solution is to allow as many opportunities as possible for students to engage in learning and demonstrate what they have learned. So, for example, since it would be unfair for a teacher to expect that every child can write a research essay, students are given a variety of other options, such as writing lyrics, creating a PowerPoint, constructing a model, making an album cover and so on. In this way, each student can engage in learning in a manner that suits her learning style and, as a result, have the opportunity to demonstrate what she's learned in a way that best showcases her domain of intelligence.

Even the physical makeup of the classroom is structured to allow students to pursue their learning styles. It's common to see elementary classrooms with desks that are paired or grouped or in a semicircle around the classroom. The purpose is to allow kids to engage each other, to hear and learn from each other's ideas and to create a lively atmosphere. With such a variety of learning styles in one classroom, it's likely that a more traditionally structured classroom would prove to be a hindrance to many of the students.

Standing in the Education Gap

Learning Styles and Self-Esteem

Paying careful attention to and supporting a student's individual learning style is also about ensuring that we are sensitive to a child's self-esteem and overall self-confidence. Perform a quick Internet search of learning styles and you will discover, time after time, claims that insist that helping a child discover her learning style will greatly increase her self-esteem. This is perhaps one of the strongest reasons why this is such a highly touted teaching approach. If a child is taught by a traditional method with little or no regard for her natural intelligence and method of learning, the end result will be a discouraged and unmotivated child with a low sense of self-worth. Once this happens, real learning can no longer take place. One of the goals of our education system, therefore, is to help every child understand and appreciate her own learning style and to understand the differences between her and her classmates. If a student lacks success and confidence, it probably has more to do with not being given the opportunity to demonstrate her area of intelligence than with any lack of effort on her part.

This particular point of view is a powerful one because it can hold much sway over our emotions. In "Learning Styles: Concepts and Evidence," an article in the journal *Psychological Science in the Public Interest*, psychologists Harold Pashler, Mark McDaniel, Doug Rohrer and Robert Bjork explain it this way:

> Another related factor that may play a role in the popularity of the learning-styles approach has to do with responsibility. If a person or a person's child is not succeeding or excelling in school, it may be more comfortable for the person to think that the educational system, not the person or the child himself or herself, is responsible. That is, rather than attribute one's lack

of success to any lack of ability or effort on one's part, it may be more appealing to think that the fault lies with instruction being inadequately tailored to one's learning style.[28]

As parents, we want to do everything we can to build our children's self-esteem. We feel the pain of their discouragement and respond with great feeling to their success and, especially, their failures. Our children, of course, are special, and we want them to know it. In a classroom, where kids pay attention to the behaviour and perceived abilities of other students, every failure can be blown up and exaggerated, putting further pressure on those kids who struggle. Learning styles seems to address our need to build up our kids. Academic struggling no longer has to be considered a lack of ability or a lack of effort; it's simply that a child hasn't yet discovered her learning style or that the classroom environment doesn't cater to her style of learning.

The Consequences

The idea that all students have a particular learning style is a compelling one. The reality, unfortunately, is a far cry from what many parents may even realize.

Chaos in the Classroom

The most obvious problem with teaching in a manner that complements every student's learning style is the number of students a teacher must manage. Even teachers who work with this goal in mind constantly search for ways to ensure that their classrooms don't became places of confusion and chaos. While arranging desks in configurations other than straight rows isn't in itself a problem, it's the purpose of the arrangement that can lead to a dysfunctional classroom. When you group students together to promote discussion or learning groups, the end result is often a lot of noise and discussion on topics other than the task at hand. Grouped desks can be useful, particularly when students are given a specific task to work on as a group after a lesson has been taught. However, far too often, teachers wrongly assume that intelligent and productive discourse will take place organically with little structure.

I distinctly remember a scenario that occurred early in my teaching days. During those years, I firmly believed that grouping desks was the best way to get students to interact, share ideas and, ultimately, become involved and motivated in their learning. More often than not, I found myself managing more than teaching and continually told myself that it was simply a lack of experience and that, given some time, advice and trial and error, my efforts would result in an orderly classroom where students would enthusiastically engage in academic activity. One day I received a card in my staff-room mailbox. It was from the principal. In it, he complimented me on the dynamic atmosphere I had created in the classroom. He had happened to glance into my classroom one day and noticed the chatter going on. He had wrongly assumed that all of this was somehow productive learning. He couldn't have been further from the truth.

Looking back, even though the administration seemed to appreciate my approach and effort, I was short-changing my students. Ironically, it wasn't until I configured my classroom in a more traditional manner that I eventually achieved greater order. While I desperately wanted to create an environment that was energetic and conducive to the discovery process, I had to face the fact that, practically speaking, it just didn't make sense to continue on the way I was going. I had to do something that actually worked.

Unequal Evaluation

On the surface, it makes sense that, if each student inherently possesses a certain learning style, then teachers must ensure that they're given every opportunity to demonstrate learning accordingly. That's one of the reasons teachers assign projects that allow for a variety of mediums. Unfortunately, the effort to give students the opportunity to pursue projects that best suit their individual learning style results in unequal grading. A child can receive just as high a grade for creating a poster as she would for completing a research essay. While the criteria in terms of content may be similar, the two simply aren't comparable. A poster, even the most creative one, may contain many elements of the required information, but an essay is a much more ambitious endeavour since information must be cited, and the essay must be well organized, cohesive and technically sound. Even for a child who enjoys writing and is generally proficient at it, writing an essay is far more labour-intensive than creating a poster. Yet in terms of grading, the poster is on equal footing with the research essay.

Given this obvious discrepancy, it isn't surprising that most students would opt to complete the easiest project. Many educators contend that students whose learning style naturally attracts them to writing would be drawn to any choice involving writing. Still others believe that as we teach kids to "learn how to learn" and instil a love for learning, they will be eager to invest time and effort in more challenging projects. These are well intentioned but completely unrealistic expectations. Even young students can calculate a return on their effort. If a good grade can be earned by completing the project that requires the least amount of time and effort, that's the one kids will choose. Students will certainly learn a valuable lesson, but not the one a teacher would hope for.

Gaps in Learning

The focus on learning styles is on the student, or the learner, instead of what is to be learned by the student. The result? Instead of teaching essential skills, teachers work to ensure that students are given opportunities to engage in their own style of learning. If certain skills must be overlooked because a child's learning style doesn't favour them, that's the route most often taken.

In our attempt to accommodate a variety of learning styles within the classroom, learning gaps often become the norm. As I mentioned, the average student will take the path of least resistance when it comes to completing assignments and projects. If that means choosing only the easiest projects, then that's what will play out over and over again. All we really end up doing is short-changing children by being much more concerned with the way they learn than what they learn.

If we don't require students to complete a well-researched, well-organized and well-written essay, at what point does a student have the opportunity to put the process of writing into practice (if research writing is ever taught at all)? Students will just move along from one grade to the next feeling good about the grades they've earned but without the ability to write a cohesive paragraph, much less a well-prepared essay.

Math is another area that has been subjected to the theory of individual learning styles. This may come as a surprise to many parents, since it seems like a subject where learning styles wouldn't factor in. Yet in the most widely used math texts in elementary schools across North America, children are seldom presented with one method for learning and successfully completing math problems. Instead, they are given a wide variety of possible ways to figure it out. While in large part this has to do with discovery learning (discussed in greater detail in Chapter 4), it's also tied to the idea that not all kids "see" math in the same way. These texts attempt to touch on as many methods as possible that suit a variety of learning styles. It isn't unusual, then, that many students end up using a calculator to find the answer to simple subtraction or multiplication questions, since this is the way in which these children learn new math concepts best.

Whether it's writing, math or any other skills-based subject, our sensitivity to individual learning styles ends up producing large gaps in learning. Armies of students end up moving from elementary to high school without the ability to string together a paragraph using correct spelling, grammar or punctuation. The scientific method is a mystery to them, and long division is a math procedure that many students simply have no idea how to correctly complete.

The Myth of Learning Skills Assessment

It's commonplace for parents to be told that their children are visual learners or auditory learners or learn best through more kinaesthetic methods. While most teachers are never formally trained to accurately assess any learning style, they are encouraged to look for the obvious signs in children. Since in today's classroom, teachers are under pressure to ensure that lessons incorporate a number of teaching approaches and modalities to meet the needs of a variety of learning styles, they can't help but observe their students and form an opinion on how each child seems to learn best. The problem is that a student's individual learning style can't actually be diagnosed, even through formal assessment.

Steven A. Stahl, a professor of reading education at the University of Georgia, states: "The reason researchers roll their eyes at learning styles is the utter failure to find that assessing children's learning styles and matching to instructional methods has any effect on their learning."[29] Stahl examined all of the research conducted on learning styles and the ways in which they were assessed and found that, in every case, there was little or no empirical evidence to support the notion that:

1. Learning styles actually exist;

2. There is a test or assessment that can determine an individual's learning style; and

3. The connection between supposed learning styles and instruction result in any improvement in learning.

Interestingly, in many of the learning-style assessment tests that were conducted, the results for a student's learning style would actually change when administered a second or third time. Why? The variables had changed. In other words, a person's learning style depended on the learning situation and the way in which the questions were asked. If, for example, an assessment determined that an individual was a visual learner, this may hold true when watching, for example, a science demonstration. However, if the same individual was attempting to learn how to properly swing a golf club, would she simply be able to watch a demonstration and then successfully swing the club and hit the golf ball straight down the fairway? It's far more likely that, in this case, the individual would need to practice swinging the golf club, being corrected as she practiced. This type of learning is associated with kinaesthetic learning. So, is this person a visual learner or a kinaesthetic learner?

In her book *Myths and Misconceptions About Teaching*, Vicki Snider aptly explains the problem:

> Learning style inventories lack validity because they don't measure ways of processing information as much as responses to particular tasks and situations. It is doubtful whether such tests would accurately predict choices learners would make under different circumstances, let alone whether or not that information is of any practical value.[30]

Given that actual research tells us that learning styles don't exist and, in particular, assessments to determine a student's learning style are completely unreliable, how much more unreliable is a classroom teacher's informal assessment? We must not confuse learning preferences with learning styles, which is what teachers often do. A lot of young students would rather watch a video than sit and practice math questions, but that doesn't make them visual learners. Preference doesn't determine if a child can learn something and shouldn't dictate how lessons are taught. Even if a teacher applies a learning-styles assessment and is trained to do so, the test only serves to give the teacher a false sense of security by providing unreliable feedback.

Why Is the Research Ignored?

If years of research on learning styles have concluded that, in fact, they don't exist, why do so many educators keep attempting to assess and create lessons that meet the variety of learning styles in the classroom? First, as unbelievable as it sounds, many teachers are completely ignorant of the research. They are so inundated by the idea that learning styles do exist through teacher conferences, workshops, textbooks and teacher-education programs that it's far easier to believe than not to. Clark, Krischner and Sweller suggest that educators are often unaware or uninterested in previous evidence that is contrary to their beliefs.[31] If so many so-called experts speak on the matter and publishers invest so much in churning out texts that support this notion, then it must be true.

Second, even for those teachers who are well-versed on what the research actually points out, learning styles just seem to feel right. Teachers will insist that they observe the differences among their students every day. If you were to observe your own interests, it appears obvious that we all respond to how information is presented in different ways. Learning styles appeal to our emotions as individuals, teachers and parents, as Snider points out:

> The appeal of learning styles is enormous, not just to teachers but to parents, too. They would prefer to label their first grader a visual learner than a poor reader or their popular, star quarterback son as a tactile/kinaesthetic learner rather than an underachiever. There is nothing inherently wrong with most of the children who struggle with school tasks. What teachers and parents do not understand is that just because children do not acquire certain academic skills naturally or without effort does not mean they are incapable. Labeling them with a learning style excuses their difficulty and ensures that they will come out of the sorting machine without the academic skills they need to become successful adults.[32]

Marc Lapointe

There Are Differences

There are differences in the way students prefer to learn. There are also differences in students' experiences, work ethic and areas of interest. All of these and more create the varying differences between levels of success in the classroom. Often the best methods for teaching new information are not always the most preferred or "fun" for students. Of course, teachers should provide variety when appropriate. Talking about a science experiment, for example, pales in comparison, in terms of learning, to teaching the scientific method and then having students actually conduct the experiment.

Learning styles, like other popular ideas in education, are based on little more than assumptive reasoning. As I briefly outlined in the introduction, many of us fall prey to the assumption that an approach or theory in education is accurate simply because it's so widely and positively talked about and, therefore, readily accepted. As parents, it's important to examine these assumptions through a more critical lens. Learning styles are a fallacy because they fail to consider context—that is, the appropriateness of a specific teaching method for a specific learning situation. Unfortunately, we've become so enamoured of the notion that our children may be struggling because the school or teacher hasn't catered to her learning style that we have failed to consider the wider implications. In the end, if we allow ourselves to buy into the notion of learning styles, all we really end up doing is crippling a child's ability to learn and taking away the opportunity for her to discover new talents and interests.

PART 2
Moving Forward

ALLOW ME TO ADDRESS THE elephant in the room before we begin the next section of this book. Are parents really qualified to help, even teach their children? If this is a question that lingers in your mind, let me put it to rest. You may not be familiar with provincial or state-mandated learning outcomes, you may know very little about teaching philosophies, you may not even feel terribly confident when it comes to helping your child with reading or math. But if you're prepared to step in and participate in your child's education, then your willingness is the best place to begin. It's your greatest qualification for this job.

I'm bringing this concern to the forefront because parents tell me all the time how unqualified they are to help their elementary-school child. You're not being asked to take over the role of the primary educator, your child's classroom teacher. We're just talking about authentic and effective support at home. All you need is some guidance, and that's essentially what this next section is about.

There are shelves of books available that address every conceivable academic issue your child could possibly face. It can be daunting, to say the least, to sift through all of the information and competing advice. My desire is to simplify that process. We will examine four main areas where parents can provide considerable help at home: math, reading, learning skills and something I like to refer to as the "intangibles." The goal is not to overwhelm you but to give you a clear picture of why these areas need so much focus and some clear guidance on how you, as the parent, can put together a practical and efficient plan for supporting your child's academics.

CHAPTER 6

Math: The Right Formula

EVERY SO OFTEN—PERHAPS IN YOUR local newspaper, a parent-oriented magazine or a television news and information program—we hear about the wonders of inquiry-based math. Stories of motivated and interested children, excited teachers and relieved and grateful parents would lead anyone to believe that math is better taught, more widely understood and more current than it has ever been. Also known as discovery-based math, this "new math" approach has advocates who claim it injects creativity, creates meaning and context and better prepares our children for the ever-changing demands of our global economy.

Discovery-based math, or for the purposes of our discussion, "new math," is by far the most prevalent and growing trend within elementary schools across North America. Direct instruction, memorization and extensive practice are largely frowned upon in favour of more "real-world" problem-solving. Children are allowed to discover answers to mathematical problems in ways that have meaning for each individual, since people can arrive at the same solution but through different methods. In a nutshell, new math focuses on the conceptual understanding of mathematics. If a child can understand a math concept or, in other words, the "whys" of math, she will grasp its relevance, achieve greater success and feel greater interest and motivation, advocates say.

Since the new-math approach concerns itself with the understanding of math concepts, there is far less emphasis on performance. This, in turn, creates a learning atmosphere free of pressure and the fear of failure. When a child can be engaged in this kind of a classroom environment, conceptual understanding comes relatively easy and, it is believed, procedural understanding will one day follow. This idea is particularly attractive to teachers and parents since so many of the struggles that students experience in math seem to have more to do with their level of confidence than their ability.

The Good News

The movement toward helping students view mathematics as something interesting and fun is a positive step. Showing kids how math is relevant in their everyday lives and beyond is well intentioned. How often have parents heard the same complaint from their kids: "How is this useful and when will I ever use this?" The new-math approach acknowledges that there are different ways to find the correct solution and gives students the opportunity to explore those ways.

Advocates of new math emphasize the need for students to develop their ability to engage in higher-order thinking. This idea takes students from the mechanical to the abstract. In other words, if students can use math to engage in more creative thinking, we can produce a whole new generation of innovators and original thinkers. Isn't this, after all, the ultimate goal of education? To turn out individuals who can positively contribute to our world in creative and innovative ways?

Educators are always thinking of ways to teach young students to become better problem-solvers. The new-math approach attempts to do just that. Instead of following something strictly formulaic, kids are presented with scenarios that encourage them to put their math skills to use. Students begin to learn that math is not just something static where problem after problem is solved but something that is useful, practical and interesting in many areas of life.

The Bad News

Like so many things in the world of elementary education, new concepts and ideas are either reactions to frustrating experiences or concepts that sound good on paper but are impractical or poorly mapped out in reality. Instead of utilizing discovery-based ideas as a way to complement and enhance more traditional methods, new math has almost completely usurped those methods.

The idea of engaging young students in activities that require a degree of critical thought is a tantalizing one. But in their enthusiasm and haste, educators have neglected to consider those steps that form the very underpinnings of the ability to engage in higher-order thinking and problem solving: the mastery of foundational math skills. Mathematician Keith Devlin remarks:

> While it sounds reasonable to suggest that understanding mathematical concepts should precede (or go along hand-in-hand with) the learning of procedural skills (such as adding fractions or solving equations), this may be (in practical terms, given the time available) impossible.... When we learn a new skill, initially we simply follow the rules in a mechanical fashion. Then, with practice we gradually become better, and as our performance improves, our understanding grows.[33]

Devlin observes a very crucial but largely ignored truth in our modern approach to teaching math: Conceptual understanding seldom precedes procedural mastery. It is, to use a familiar colloquialism, like putting the cart before the horse. Somehow we've been fooled into believing that our children can become proficient math students without ever receiving the very tools necessary to successfully solve math problems.

The ability to add, subtract, multiply and divide are the most basic and essential tools in math. In order for children to make use of these tools, they must first master them through direct instruction, practice and repetition. Yet in countless elementary classrooms across North America, this approach is demonized. The belief is that practice and repetition can only result in bored and frustrated children. Furthermore, supporters of new math insist that no new learning comes as a result of practice and repetition. This is a complete misunderstanding as to the purpose of practice and repetition. It isn't about new learning—it's about reinforcing what has been taught. This forms the basis upon which new learning and understanding can take place in future lessons.

Somehow our system of education has concluded that basic skills and conceptual understanding are mutually exclusive. What's more, given that conceptual understanding and, therefore, higher-order thinking skills are deemed much more desirable than basic skills, any attempt to teach and reinforce fundamental math skills has been mostly abandoned. Hung-His Wu, a professor of mathematics at the University of California Berkley, observes:

> "Facts vs. higher ordering thinking" is another example of a false choice that we often encounter these days, as if thinking of any sort—high or low—could exist outside of content knowledge. In mathematics education, this debate takes the form of "basic skills

or conceptual understanding." This bogus dichotomy would seem to arise from a common misconception of mathematics held by a segment of the public and the education community: that the demand for precision and fluency in the execution of basic skills in school mathematics runs counter to the acquisition of conceptual understanding. The truth is that in mathematics, skills and understanding are completely intertwined. In most cases, the precision and fluency in the execution of the skills are the requisite vehicles to convey the conceptual understanding. There is not "conceptual understanding" and "problem-solving skill" on the one hand and "basic skills" on the other. Nor can one acquire the former without the latter.[34]

Why New Math?

If the new-math approach, with its focus on inquiry and discovery-based methods, is so ineffective in providing elementary students with the essential skills they need, why is it still championed by so many educators?

A Reaction to Rote Learning

As I mention throughout this book, seldom is the right balance struck in the realm of elementary education when it comes to teaching approaches. Not so long ago, math was taught in a much more regimented way. The concern with this method of teaching was that those who didn't grasp it would inevitably feel discouraged and, as a consequence, develop a definite dislike for the subject. Educators, in an attempt to find ways to motivate children, decided to do away with what they perceived as a restricted method of learning and go in the opposite direction.

Mathematician John Mighton observes that "too often in the math wars we tend to throw out the good with the bad and we swing wildly back and forth between competing trends."[35] The problem with new math is not so much the idea but its insistence that all other approaches, particularly those that involve direct instruction, a focus on procedural mastery and practice are considered invalid. Instead of examining the strengths and weaknesses of a certain approach or philosophy, our education system simply reacts, devises new ideas that have been neither tested nor, in some cases, well thought through and then implements them. Such is the case with the discovery-based approach that is so prominent in new math.

It Seems to Engage Students

Whenever we think of what an interested or engaged student looks like, we picture a child who is actively participating, asking questions and displaying a general level of enthusiasm for what she's learning. It's not surprising that for elementary teachers who lack both an expertise and an enthusiasm for math, the traditional methods of teaching math are simply boring. Teachers perceive that their students are not engaged, not interested and therefore not learning.

The new-math approach uses terms like "reflect," "explore," "explain," "elaborate" and, of course "engage." All of these words clearly suggest that some form of active learning is taking place. Direct instruction, memorization and practice are, by contrast, very passive activities. Ask any advocate of the new-math approach, and he or she will insist that math should be an "active" learning activity. All of this sounds very promising—but we gain something that sounds good while losing those methods of teaching math that actually work.

Many Teachers Don't Know Any Better

As mentioned in Chapter 2, most elementary school teachers don't have any formal training in mathematics. There are, in fact, a lot of elementary teachers who have a decidedly negative attitude toward math. These educators typically support the use of a discovery-based math program because they lack the expertise and experience to know better. In addition, the fact that new math simply sounds more engaging is enough to draw their support. Among other things, the new-math approach is regarded as an "authentic" approach to teaching math. When we associate this word with the discovery-based method of new math, the meaning becomes unmistakable: This approach to math is genuine and all others aren't. What teacher would dare challenge this bold suggestion? If a teacher doesn't have expertise in math and is, in fact, a little uncomfortable teaching it, she would never venture to express any criticism. By skipping over the direct instruction of foundational algorithms in elementary math, the many holes in the teacher's level of understanding and expertise can be easily avoided.

I have seen personal examples of this with my own children. Struggling at times with some of the content in his math textbook—decidedly discovery-based—my son found little help from his teacher, who often insisted that he just had to "work it out." Upon visiting the teacher to see if I might get a better understanding of my child's struggles, I found an individual who was warm and enthusiastic but had a vague notion as to the teaching of foundational skills like long division. As I inquired more deeply about his understanding of the math program he was using, the teacher proceeded to provide me with a list of the very phrases that I have been so critical about: "It's more authentic" and "It's more student-centred and hands-on" and, of course, "It's a great program because it really helps kids think more deeply about math instead of just memorizing things." I walked away wondering at the irony of what he shared with me. In our attempts to ensure that kids really understand math, not just memorize multiplication tables and the like, we've caused our teachers to understand very little of what they're teaching in math and the reasons for it.

The best elementary math teachers are those who clearly understand the shortcomings of new math. While not all of them started out having much expertise in math, they took it upon themselves to dig deeper and not only become proficient at arithmetic and algebra themselves but also learn exactly how it can be taught effectively. Their goal isn't to undermine the new-math program, since it is really the only resource provided to them and their students, but to find ways for more so-called traditional methods to complement the methods of new math.

The Right Method for the Information Age

Teachers and parents have been fooled into believing that, in our modern, fast-paced world, traditional approaches to math education are out-dated. Consider the following statement from Deb Russell, an experienced teacher and school principal who writes about mathematics for About.com, regarding math in the modern age:

> Societal needs have changed, thus math has changed. We are now in an information age with technology paving the way. It is no longer enough to do computations; that's what calculators and computers are for. Math today requires decisions about which

keys to punch in and which graph to use, not how to construct them! Math requires creative problem solving techniques. Today's math requires real-life problems to solve, a skill highly prized by employers today. Math requires knowing when and how to use the tools to assist in the problem solving process. This happens as early as pre-kindergarten when children seek counters, an abacus, blocks and a variety of other manipulatives.[36]

The sentiment shared by this particular educator is a common argument used by advocates of new math. Consider the premise that, somehow, "math has changed." This suggests that mathematics is a relative truth and its validity changes with the times. Even if we were to agree that, perhaps, the ways in which we use math have evolved with our technology, it in no way means that a person can magically gain an understanding of complex math without first having a firm grasp of basic but foundational skills. I would suggest that, in an information age where technology is constantly advancing, a greater emphasis on acquiring foundational skills is *more* important than ever—not less.

The Inconvenient Truth

As alluring as the new-math approach may sound to both teachers and parents, it falls short—far short—of ensuring that elementary students learn math with skill, accuracy and confidence. Instead of the bright promise of successful and confident math students, we get a reality that's far less attractive.

Watered-Down Mathematics

We have sacrificed procedural mastery for conceptual understanding and chosen to ignore the link between the two. As a result, math in elementary school lacks rigour, thoroughness and precision. Since the goal of the teacher is to help students discover a variety of methods in order to successfully complete various math problems, far more value is placed on a student's effort rather then accuracy. While effort is certainly important, it's only one component that leads to the eventual mastery and understanding of math concepts.

As we'll see shortly, teaching math in an incremental manner is one of the vital characteristics of an effective math education. Learning math incrementally by its nature takes time, but it ensures that a child not only masters and understands the material but also is fully prepared to build upon what has been learned. This is one of the essentials of teaching math, and there's no getting around the fact that it's thorough. Unfortunately, it's this very fact that causes educators to be critical of any math program that's so rigorous. It can be hard work, it can take time, and performance is the final measure of whether or not a student has learned and understood the work. As many educators see it, this allows little room for building a child's self-esteem; therefore, the method is rejected wholeheartedly.

Too Much Information

Proponents of new math argue that mathematical concepts won't make sense to young students unless you present them with the big picture. The idea is that the big picture will demonstrate the relevance of the concept. If young students understand the "whys" of a certain math concept, that will naturally lead to a desire to learn it. Procedures, then, only get in the way of learning the overall concept. Educators argue that if we teach children procedures instead of helping them grasp the relevance of the concept, then they will only see math as a series of dull, disconnected actions.

The ultimate goal for any math student is to eventually grasp math concepts. The problem with teaching concepts or the big picture as a stand-alone approach is that students can easily become overwhelmed by the sheer amount of information that they would need to process in order to eventually come to understanding. Mighton pinpoints this problem:

> Anyone who has taught children knows that it is not always practical to start with the big picture, because the human mind can hold only so much information at a time, and an overwhelmed student can shut down or easily be discouraged.[37]

Should we wonder, then, that so many middle- and high-school students struggle with algebra? Algebra, as a concept, involves a variety of mathematical components, including the ability to successfully calculate relatively simple and basic multiplication and long division. Yet in a vast number of elementary math classrooms across North America, long division in particular is largely ignored. The argument is that it takes too much time for students to complete long division questions and, with regard to algebra, it only gets in the way of understanding the larger concept.

When we break down math into smaller incremental parts or procedures, we allow for students to take in information in manageable pieces. Yes, a young student may forge ahead without yet seeing or grasping the big picture, but like the parts of a jigsaw puzzle, the pieces inevitably fit together so that the student can eventually see the whole concept. Along the way, she has mastered integral procedures that allow her to answer complex algebraic equations with success and confidence.

High Degree of Frustration

Discovery-based math can be just plain confusing and frustrating. An article from *Maclean's* magazine examined the state of elementary math education in Canada and made this observation:

> Changes in the curriculum-which have rolled cumulatively over the past decade and intensified in recent years-had sounded so promising: instead of stifling them with rote memorization and rigid methods, children are to use their own learning style to explore mathematical knowledge and conceptualize innovative solutions to complex problems, preparing them for an ever-changing tech-based economy. But the execution of this vision hasn't been so idealistic. Instead of building a generation of math whizzes, it's creating a Tower of Babel, where teachers can't understand textbooks, students can't understand teachers, and parents and children have no idea what the other is talking about.[38]

It's no wonder that, with so much confusion even among classroom teachers, the new-math approach does little, if anything, to build the confidence, much less the understanding, of so many young students. Add to that the general level of frustration parents feel, and what you're left with is something that is a far cry from the idealistic vision of confident and competent math students. It is, like the Tower of Babel, a confusing mess.

So, What Is Important?

Here's the bottom line: All children in elementary school, before they advance to high school, should be proficient in arithmetic. Arithmetic, quite simply, is the branch of mathematics concerned with numerical calculations: addition, subtraction, multiplication and division. Mathematician W. Stephen Wilson, writing in the journal *Educational Leadership*, explains:

> Like it or not, arithmetic is the foundation of mathematics. Studying slides, flips, and turns year after year (as many state standards stipulate) will not prepare a student for college mathematics.... Students must study arithmetic. The standard algorithms for whole numbers are the only really big theorems that students can be taught in elementary school. It is deep, beautiful and powerful mathematics. Master these algorithms with understanding, and you're ready to go.[39]

At first glance, parents might consider the mastery of arithmetic to be too simple a solution. However, it's new math, with its vague notions of conceptual understanding and problem-solving, that has muddied the waters. In the end it seems that no one, not even the average elementary-school teacher, is certain what students should learn in math and why.

By focusing on arithmetic in the elementary years, we make the learning of math simple. I don't mean that learning math becomes easy and no longer requires a degree of hard work and concentration. It's simple in the sense that our goals are clear and we can see a definite progression between what a young student learns in the present and the more complex math she will learn in the future. It also means that, for teachers and parents, there is a common, understandable approach. We can avoid the Tower of

Babel effect and, particularly for parents, provide reliable support and help for our children.

With all this in mind, there are what I consider to be four cornerstones for teaching math in elementary school. These ideas aren't new and revolutionary, but they are the most effective methods for helping young students master arithmetic. Proponents of new math would likely scoff at these ideas, since they aren't cutting-edge. But new and cutting-edge isn't my concern—it's what works that should be of primary importance to parents and educators.

Cornerstone #1: Direct Instruction

Despite new math's discovery-based approach, which holds to the belief that the teacher is more of a facilitator than an instructor, students require direct instruction from the teacher. The procedure must be taught directly to the child. The premise is that students are not the experts and, this being the case, require the expertise of a teacher. Through direct instruction, we ensure that students learn the procedures correctly the first time.

Cornerstone #2: Practice

I am always amazed at the inability of young, struggling students to make the connection between a lack of success and a lack of practice. Particularly in math, practice is absolutely essential. However, we buy into the notion that it bores students, and therefore it's a learning tool that should be avoided. Even more amazing is our immediate acceptance that practice is absolutely necessary to improve in music or sports. Could you imagine a piano teacher who chose to teach piano as a concept, allowing her young piano pupils to discover the keys and notes on the piano?

After some time, would we wonder why our child still couldn't play even a simple song even though she almost never practiced? We wouldn't only think this was absurd, we would never bring our child to that piano teacher again. So why should it be any different with math?

Cornerstone #3: Repetition

To many educators, repetition is like a four-letter word and, therefore, best avoided. "Drill and kill" is the term most widely used by teachers to deride any approach that requires young students to memorize and recite information. With the new-math approach, it's rare to find students memorizing their multiplication tables. Instead, they are taught how to count in groups on their fingers. While this may be a useful practice in teaching primary-grade students, it's disconcerting to find kids in Grade 8 and 9 attempting to figure out what 5 x 7 is on their fingers (and only if they don't have a calculator handy).

In order to ensure that something is so ingrained in our memory that we can recall it with little difficulty and put it to immediate use, we must repeat it over and over again. Advocates of new math would state that it's not repetition that makes something memorable; it's memorable experiences or knowledge that is built upon existing knowledge. They're right, but they fail to consider that a memorable "experience" in math does not equal mastery, and in order to build upon existing knowledge, the existing knowledge must first be present and accurate. If a child can't, for example, multiply simple numbers without the use of a calculator, is her existing knowledge reliable enough that we can build upon it with more complex math formulas?

Cornerstone #4: Incremental Steps

Math, particularly in elementary school, must be learned incrementally. This means that basic procedures are mastered before moving into more complex procedures. In addition, each lesson and each unit connects to the lesson or unit before. There is a common thread throughout all math lessons. When your child is able to learn a math procedure incrementally, the information comes in easy-to-digest amounts.

Learning incrementally also involves review. Just because a child may learn a new procedure doesn't mean she should move on to the next lesson and forget what was just learned. Since each step builds upon the next, review is an important part of the process. Review allows a child to solidify her learning and see how new lessons or procedures build from that. In this way, nothing is entirely "new" to your child; it's simply more complex and advanced.

Incremental learning is also extremely helpful for parents, especially those who are a little intimidated by math or feel that their skills are rusty. It's much easier to grasp smaller steps than relearn entire concepts. If you feel you are simply not "wired" to do math, you'll be pleasantly surprised at how procedures that once seemed tough to understand are now relatively easy to grasp. In fact, don't be surprised to find your own confidence increase as your child's does.

A Parent's Role

While the situation in the classroom may shake your confidence a little, parents can have a real, lasting and positive impact on their child's mastery of math. This doesn't mean that Mom and Dad should take over the role of their child's teacher, but they can ensure that their son or daughter has the foundational skills necessary for succeeding in the elementary-school classroom and, ultimately, in high school and beyond.

First Things First

Let me be clear: The ultimate goal for your child is to eventually engage in complex math problems involving those skills that would be considered higher-order thinking skills—in other words, to one day have the ability to fully grasp math concepts and to apply the correct formulas in order to successfully solve complicated, multistep problems. This is, I believe, the goal of the new-math approach as well. While it's a worthwhile objective and one that I fully endorse, new math's discovery approach gets ahead of itself and ignores the need to master foundational mathematics.

It's imperative that children master addition, subtraction, multiplication and long division—without the use of a calculator. It's important to mention that, when learning math, a child's grade level should not serve as the starting point. Instead, it should be your son or daughter's ability that dictates where to begin. While it isn't exactly practical to design the classroom curriculum around this idea, it's easily done at home. This means that, even if your child is in Grade 7, it may be necessary to review and practice addition and subtraction—seemingly more basic math—if she has trouble correctly completing calculations using addition or subtraction. In fact, in my experience, it isn't unusual to come across students in Grade 8 or even Grade 9 who can't subtract multi-digit numbers without the use of a calculator. By the same token, your child may be more advanced than the average child in her grade, and it may be appropriate to begin reviewing and practicing long division, for example, as early as Grade 2 or 3.

Time

One of the biggest objections parents have to actually teaching their children arithmetic is that it would take too much time. Coupled with the first objection, a comment about how "it's the school's job to teach my child" closely follows. If your child is struggling in math, then time is what's required—that is the unavoidable truth. While it's the job of our schools to educate our kids, it should be clear at this point why, as parents, we can't simply sit back and hope that our kids are thoroughly and successfully educated.

Since one of the keys to teaching math effectively is to teach it incrementally, the amount of time involved doesn't need to be a huge commitment. In reality, it should take between 15 and 30 minutes a day to teach your child arithmetic. The key, however, is consistency. As parents, our goal is to teach foundational, procedural skills incrementally and in a way that builds upon the previous day's lesson. By keeping the time relatively short, we allow our son or daughter to remember bite-sized pieces that eventually make up the whole. As I've mentioned, one of the reasons kids have so much trouble is that whenever math is taught as a concept, there is simply too much information to digest.

Besides consistency, your approach should also involve mastery. Before you move forward, your child should have mastered the procedures that you have attempted to teach her. While you don't want to linger on the same lesson forever, you shouldn't concern yourself with strict timelines. Mastery should come before advancement.

Resources

There are literally hundreds of math resources offered by a variety of websites, publishers and individuals that claim their program will help your child become a better math student. Some are excellent; many aren't. When considering which resource to use, make sure you ask the following questions:

- *Does the program teach math in incremental steps?* It's not unusual for math programs, like texts used in most elementary schools, to bombard student with reams of conceptual information. If this is the case, keep looking.

- *What is the teaching philosophy of the program?* Does it advocate a discovery approach to math or does it encourage procedural skills over concepts? Typically, inquiry or discovery-based math programs are very wordy, since the questions are meant to somehow promote greater critical thought. This can be confusing for both the students and the parents. Our goal is to keep it simple but effective, and so a program like this should be avoided.

- *Does the program utilize a common-sense approach to teaching math?* There are countless math programs that claim to use a multisensory approach or a kinaesthetic approach that involves movement, and there are many others that, when you examine them with a critical eye, seem too complex and experimental to actually make much sense. Utilize what has been proven to work and walk away from anything that sounds too good to be true, no matter how convincing it may sound. I often liken unrealistic claims to improve your child's learning through dubious means to the various weight-loss products peddled on late-night television or in magazine ads. Most of us realize how unlikely it is that, by applying a special cream or ingesting a certain pill, we'll become leaner and fitter. Good old-fashioned exercise and smart eating habits are the tried and true method to reaching your fitness goals. Be just as critical about suspect math programs, no matter how tempted you may be to find an easier alternative.

- *Does the program cover math from kindergarten to Grade 7 or 8?* If you've discovered an excellent math program that meets your criteria, you'll want to continue using it as your child progresses. If the program only focuses on a single math skill, such as adding, or is limited in terms of how it advances a child's skills, you may want to search for one that isn't so limited. However, even if the program has its limits in terms of advancing your child along, it may be a very effective resource for a specific purpose and still worth using.

My goal is to give you guidelines on how to choose a math program to use at home, not to scrutinize specific programs. That being said, there are two resources that I believe represent excellent examples of the kind of math program I would encourage parents to consider: JUMP Math and Saxon Math. Both programs meet most or all of the criteria I've outlined. In terms of after-school home use, you may find that JUMP Math is more practical and less costly. Teacher's guides can be downloaded at no cost, and the workbooks are reasonably priced and can be purchased from online bookstores like Amazon and even warehouse-type stores like Costco. Saxon Math, while an excellent program, is designed for use in the classroom and for homeschoolers.

What's Wrong With Using Calculators?

The use of calculators in elementary school can be a touchy subject. On the one hand, there are those who feel that by allowing students to use calculators, we can decrease their stress level and increase their interest in math. This is particularly true when students are working on more complex word problems. A calculator can help a student devote all of her attention to solving the word problem instead of dividing her attention between the calculations and the word problem. On the other hand, there are those who see calculators as a barrier to learning, since students can easily become dependent on the devices and lose the ability to solve simple calculations on paper or in their heads.

Both sides of this debate have legitimate arguments. However, it's clear that, overall, students' basic computational skills are lacking. This problem begins in elementary school, thanks to the way in which the new-math approach focuses on discovery through problem-solving. Since students have to split their attention between deciphering wordy questions, solving word-problems and completing basic calculations, computational skills are neglected. When the focus is on conceptual understanding, procedural skills not only take a back seat, they're often forgotten. Adding, subtracting, multiplying and dividing are all completed with the use of a calculator, since doing them without one not only takes up more time, it takes the focus away from grasping the overall concept.

There are few reasons for elementary students up to Grade 8 to be using calculators. While mathematical concepts may become more advanced, basic calculation skills are more than enough to help students successfully solve most math problems. Recently I had a conversation with a student in Grade 9. She mentioned how much she was struggling with math that year. She explained that, in elementary and middle school, math was easy for her and she consistently earned an A. She gave me an example of her current struggles where, on a recent test, her teacher would not allow calculators to be used because the calculations were, in the mind of the teacher, relatively simple. The student told me that much of the test required her to solve long-division problems involving decimals. She said she had never been taught long division and, to make matters worse, dividing numbers with decimals was an impossible task.

Students who have been taught how to add, subtract, multiply and divide without a calculator are rarely thrown off or unprepared when they don't have a calculator. In fact, it would be relatively easy for a student in Grade 6 or 7 to complete a long-division question involving decimals if she was taught properly. As parents, we might find the argument for the use of calculators in elementary school convincing. But why would we not want to arm our children with every academic advantage as they advance to high school and beyond? Calculators in the elementary grades, while a definite timesaver and less of a headache for teachers, lead to a detrimental dependency later on.

For many parents, the prospect of helping a child master foundational math skills can be daunting. Math, more than any other core subject, has the tendency to intimidate people. For many of these individuals, the fear stems from their own negative experiences or overall poor performance in math in elementary and high school. But teaching your child arithmetic doesn't have to be a scary undertaking. Yes, it may mean that you will have to refresh your knowledge of math or even relearn some procedures. It may even mean that, from time to time, your child may not understand or advance as quickly as you think she should, and as a result, you may see your efforts as fruitless. But take it from a former English major turned math teacher: You can effectively learn, master and teach math to your elementary child if you're focused and incremental in your approach and, especially, patient with your child along the way. Who knows, you might, like so many parents I've worked with, actually find math to be an enjoyable experience the second time around—especially as you begin to see your efforts have a positive influence in your child's success in math.

CHAPTER 7

Understanding Reading

THE IMPORTANCE OF LITERACY CAN'T be overstated. Literacy allows a person to communicate, to acquire knowledge, to understand the complexity of a problem or issue and simply to enjoy a good story. It crosses over into so many areas of everyday life. In school, it is the very foundation of learning. If a child isn't literate, she won't grasp the instructions in a math text, interpret facts and events in science or social studies or find enjoyment in reading a novel.

There are few things more frustrating for a parent of a struggling elementary student then being told by the classroom teacher that, in order for the child to improve in her reading fluency and comprehension, she should be encouraged to read more. In other words, if the child is immersed in an environment rich in literature, she will naturally become a student who not only can make sense of the words on the page but also can fully grasp the meaning of a wide variety of texts and books. The problem is that this advice rarely, if ever, makes an impact. Parents will read to their children and with their children. They will introduce them to scores of books from age-appropriate picture books to levelled readers to comics. And still the door to literacy and reading comprehension will not open.

Teaching children to read is probably one of the most important—and difficult—endeavours teachers or parents can undertake. We are led to believe that reading is a natural process because we wrongly compare it to the way a toddler develops speech or the ability to stand and walk. Learning how to read, despite what many teachers have been taught to believe, is not a natural process. As education critic E. D. Hirsch, Jr., writes in his book *The Knowledge Deficit*:

> There is little in the human organism that prepares us naturally for alphabetic reading and writing (decoding and encoding), which have been very late and rare attainments of civilization. The inherent unnaturalness of learning to read is part of the reason that it is at first so difficult and, for many, so painful.[40]

For a child, learning to read is hard work. Is it any wonder, then, that some parents begin to worry about their child's ability or intelligence when our elementary schools tell us that it should come naturally?

In elementary education today, there is a battle going on over the best approach to teaching students reading and reading comprehension. There is, understandably, a lot of confusion among parents; they are given a lot of advice, but it adds up to very little progress when it comes to a child's ability to read and understand what she's reading. On the one hand, we're told that reading is a natural process where, given time and enough exposure to various forms of literature, a child will eventually catch on. On the other, the sooner a child begins to decode letters and their sounds, the better. In the meantime, parents feel almost powerless to do anything since, with all of the edu-babble going on, they feel unqualified and uninformed.

Reading Education in Today's Classroom

As I've discussed throughout this book, teaching in today's elementary classroom leans toward a student-centred approach. Our education system generally views reading—or more specifically, the learning of reading—to be a natural process. This means that children only need to be immersed in an environment of reading and to be given the opportunity to read what is meaningful to them. Literacy, both in terms of decoding and comprehension, develops in its own, natural way for each child.

This approach to reading is known as the whole-language approach. While some educators claim it's a relatively new and improved approach to the teaching of reading, it isn't. In fact, the whole-language approach has been around for decades and has been known by other names, such as "look and say," "global," and more recently "sight word." Those who advocate the whole-language approach believe that words should not be decoded or broken down into their individual sounds and combinations of sounds. Instead, the goal of reading education is for children to obtain meaning from the words and understand the meaning of a word, phrase or sentence in context.

Sight Words

Since there is very little, if any, emphasis on the decoding of words, children in the primary grades are taught how to recognize the most common or high-frequency words they will encounter. It's not unusual for teachers to introduce sight words that are considered developmentally appropriate for the early years in elementary school. Terms like "pre-primer" and "primer" are common and represent lists of words that preschool and kindergarten children should learn to recognize first. Recognition, of course, involves memorization. In some circles, sight words are known as Dolch lists, an inventory of words proposed by E. W. Dolch as being the most commonly occurring words in children's books. His list of 220 "service words" was compiled in the 1930s. Since sight words are supposed to comprise over 75 percent of what is printed in most children's literature, the belief is that the better a child memorizes and recognizes these words, the greater her reading ability will be.

The arguments for the teaching of sight words can be persuasive. Children, particularly those just learning to read, seem to have a natural tendency for memorizing words. If this is a child's natural function, then why discourage it? In the case of the Dolch list, it seems reasonable that, if a child can memorize this list of words, and these words comprise three quarters of the words printed in much of children's literature, then the teaching of reading is that much easier. In addition, having young students recognize sight words helps to avoid the inevitable problems associating with decoding English words where there are rules and then there are exceptions to those rules. While these arguments may sound convincing, the truth is that teaching young children to read through the memorization and recognition of sight words is an inefficient and ineffective process. Sebastian Wren, creator of the literacy research site BalancedReading.com, notes:

> Clearly this strategy for learning new words is maladaptive. Children memorize a word that is highly dependent upon context, and because most words share many visual features with many other words, children who attempt to memorize words as wholes tend to confuse words. Moreover, there is a limit as to how many words children can memorize -- while most competent readers have a reading vocabulary of around

50,000 words, children who memorize words as wholes are only capable of learning a maximum of about 5,000 words in isolation.[41]

Cueing

The three-cueing system is an approach to the teaching of reading or, more specifically, word recognition that involves three cues or prompts for young students to utilize. The first cue involves guessing the meaning of an unknown word based on the context of the story. The second involves syntax—if a child continues to struggle with the meaning of a word, she's encouraged to observe things like word order, sentence patterns and verb tenses as further clues. The last cue, considered to be the one of last resort, is phonological; a child is encouraged to try to sound out the word if she has failed to figure out its meaning through context or syntax.

As a child begins to tackle more complex texts and books, she will inevitably encounter more and more challenging words. For advanced readers, particularly adults who are proficient readers, cueing seems to make sense. It's not unusual that as we read and come across words that we're unfamiliar with, we attempt to derive their meaning from the context of the passages before and after. However, what we might fail to consider is that there are many variables that go into finding the meaning of a new word. When it comes to children, particularly those whose proficiency in reading is in the relatively early stages, cueing turns into more of a guessing game. Like sight words, cueing as a method for young readers to decipher the meaning of individual words is both unproductive and largely fruitless. In *The Science of Reading: A Handbook*, reading researchers Catherine E. Snow and Connie Juel write:

Numerous studies in the 1980s indicated use of context for word identification is both inefficient and minimally useful. At best, for example, adult readers can accurately predict one of four words in text, and the most accurate predictions are of function words. Skilled readers can only accurately predict one in ten content words, and predicting words takes longer than just looking at the word.[42]

If studies have shown that discovering the meaning of unknown words through examining the context of a passage has minimal results with adults, then why should we expect the results to be far more profound with young children?

Prior Knowledge

The use of prior knowledge and experience is a teaching strategy designed to help students improve their reading comprehension. The idea is that, as students read, they are constantly making connections to the things they already know in order to understand the meaning of the text. By helping students to activate their prior knowledge, it's said that they become more independent and active readers. This, in turn, develops their metacognitive skills or, in other words, their ability to think critically about what they're reading.

It's true that knowledge is one of the most important keys in effective reading comprehension (which we'll discuss a little later in the chapter). However, when it comes to the whole-language approach, it's simply assumed that a child's knowledge or previous experience is sufficient. In an education system that encourages a learner or student-centred approach to teaching, true knowledge is tossed aside in favour of discovery. Discovery of concepts or knowledge, as I've pointed out time and again, can often be inaccurate or irrelevant. Coupled with this is the fact that creating a classroom environment that caters exclusively to a discovery approach is a very inefficient use of time. The time it takes to discover accurate, reliable and relevant knowledge, therefore, is a slow process if it ever takes place at all.

Student-Centred

Student-centred reading education can involve many elements. Typically, it gives "ownership" of the learning to the individual student. In other words, whether it's through small-group discussions or various "reflective" exercises that are facilitated by the classroom teacher, students are encouraged to make connections, devise strategies and create their own reasoning in order to increase their ability to read, grasp and think more deeply about a specific piece of writing. It's not unusual that students are given the opportunity to choose their own books. Teachers will pass along various strategies that students can take advantage of in order to increase their fluency and comprehension but, for the most part, kids follow the habits and routines of reading as they see fit. Since the whole-language approach is largely student-centred, it's argued that children are more motivated to read, to improve and to engage in more complex texts.

Student-centred learning, particularly when it comes to learning how to read with fluency and comprehension, is a dubious practice. While discussion groups may give the appearance of active learning, it can be more akin to the blind leading the blind unless there is direct intervention by the classroom teacher. When we allow students to collaborate on the meaning of new words based on their understanding of the context of the book, chapter or passage, we are basically encouraging students to guess and to put their faith in the guesswork of their peers. This type of student-centred activity further slows the process of real learning.

The Path to Reading Mastery

In reality, there is no one approach that effectively teaches students how to read. Let me be clear: There is an effective path that should be followed, but becoming an effective reader, one who not only knows how to decode the written word but can comprehend it, involves many strategies. In the world of reading education there are often two camps: phonics vs. whole language. Both have their place, so the question is not necessarily which approach is better, but which is most appropriate at specific times in a student's reading development—in other words, a balanced approach.

As I've mentioned before, when it comes to elementary education, our system is prone to extremes. This means that any method considered old and traditional is typically thrown out in its entirety, and more so-called progressive ideas end up taking its place. Whole-language has a place but only at a certain point in a student's reading development. Unfortunately, it is an approach to reading education that is often used at every level of development. Instead, effective teaching of reading should follow a logical path where a child starts with the intentional decoding of words and progresses to the full comprehension of a passage, article, paper, text or novel.

Phonics

Phonics, quite simply, is the relationship between sounds and letters. At its most basic level, having a young child learn the alphabet and each letter's corresponding sound is a form of phonics instruction. As a child progresses, she learns the sounds of long and short vowels and then letters in combination. This advances until the student begins to read passages of writing by sounding out the letter combinations in the text until a word is recognized. Strictly speaking, it's the process of decoding written language. As a child becomes more and more familiar with the sounds of letter combinations through frequent practice, her ability to read will become more fluid and, as a consequence, she will increase her working vocabulary.

The teaching of phonics is the most effective way to help young students learn to read. A study on phonemic awareness instruction published in *Reading Research Quarterly* states:

> [The] benefits of phonemic awareness instruction were replicated multiple times across experiments and thus provided solid support for the claim that PA instruction is more effective than alternative forms of instruction or no instruction in teaching PA in helping children acquire reading and spelling skills.[43]

Especially in the primary years, phonics is far superior in the teaching of reading over sight words in at least one distinct way: the use of working memory. By having children memorize a list of words, we challenge the limits of their working memory while providing little in the way of parsing out new words that aren't included on the sight-word list. Phonics provides an incremental system for decoding words, starting with the English alphabet. By allowing a child to learn and identify letter sounds and then, later, letter sounds in combination, we can avoid overwhelming her working memory. We no longer limit her ability to read simple sentences to a list of sight words but, instead, give her the tools to decode any words she encounters.

Phonics represents the beginning of reading. The whole-language approach, to put it bluntly, gets ahead of itself. In one sense, the ultimate purpose of reading education is for children to comprehend what they read and think critically about it. Whole language seeks to inject comprehension from the beginning. That is perhaps its greatest weakness. Reading involves the mastery of decoding skills first. The effective decoding of written language is the foundation and the starting point of solid reading comprehension. As Jeanne S. Chall writes in *The Academic Achievement Challenge:*

> If phonics is not learned early, phonological factors may indeed interfere with the use of language and reasoning in reading development. For older students with reading problems, language and cognitive difficulties are not always the central factor; rather, the difficulty may still be mainly with phonics, which leads to further difficulty with fluency and comprehension.[44]

Teaching the ability to decode before we concern a student with comprehension is absolutely integral to effective reading later in elementary school and beyond.

Phonics as the Gateway to Comprehension

Phonics instruction serves as the gateway to reading comprehension. Study after study has revealed that the reason so many older children struggle with their comprehension has to do with the fact that their phonological, or decoding, skills are lacking. Researcher Kate Nation, in her contribution to *The Science of Reading: A Handbook*, explains:

> It is well established that children's phonological skills are intimately related to the development of literacy

and a considerable body of evidence points to core phonological deficits characterizing individuals with poor reading.... On this view, comprehension problems are a consequence of a child being unable to set up or sustain a phonological representation of verbal information when reading.[45]

There are schools that incorporate phonics into their reading programs. However, for the most part, the instruction isn't explicit and is often done in combination with various whole-language approaches. The end result is that phonics instruction is watered down. Our education system concerns itself so much with comprehension and critical thinking in its youngest students that, even when teachers and administrators have little choice but to admit the importance of phonics, it is still largely avoided.

Why, with so much evidence staring educators in the face, do our schools not explicitly teach phonics to students from the start of their reading education? Chall suggests a possible explanation:

> Proponents of these reforms [those that put the emphasis on meaning] claimed that reading for understanding right from the start was the best way to learn to read and to become a proficient reader as an adult. They abhorred rote learning. Concern with the phonological aspects of reading was seen then—as it is now, unfortunately—by whole-language proponents as pulling the reader away from understanding and toward rote learning. Therefore, it was to be avoided.... Learning phonics was viewed as dull and dreary and as discouraging a wide range of reading and a lifetime love of it.[46]

Phonics is work, there's little doubt about it. But what else should we expect when taking a child who has no ability to read and introducing her to an utterly new world? Since, as I've established, reading isn't a natural process, the work involved simply can't—and shouldn't—be avoided. Reading for understanding and meaning sounds and feels so right and profound. Decoding and, more specifically, phonics don't have the attraction and allure associated with critical thinking. Our concern that students might find the decoding of language too boring shouldn't be one of the guiding principles in teaching them. Unfortunately, modern-day approaches to reading education cater to those exact attitudes.

Knowledge

While phonics serves as the starting point on a child's path to becoming an effective reader, it doesn't encompass the whole of reading instruction. Even students who show a wonderful proficiency for decoding can, and often do, struggle with comprehension in later grades. One of the elements of the whole-language approach is the belief that students can understand the meaning of an unknown word in two ways: by examining the context of the passage or story and by tapping into prior knowledge. This is where the whole-language approach, at least in part, gets it right. Once a child can decode and begin to read with fluency, the type of texts and books she reads will, naturally, become more advanced. She will inevitably come across new words, and even though she may be able to read them through decoding, she may not understand their meaning. That's where knowledge comes in.

If a student has more knowledge of a variety of subjects, she will have a greater ability to understand the context of a passage and ultimately have the ability to decipher the meaning of new words. The problem, then, is not with the soundness of this theory but with students' lack of knowledge. For example, I have a brother who knows the language of technology. By comparison, I'm a complete neophyte. There are times when my brother and I talk about a specific piece of software, or I need help with some computer glitch, and I can barely grasp what he's trying to explain. He's speaking English, but his knowledge in this realm far exceeds my own. I'm sure that, at times, my brother is confounded by my lack of understanding, especially considering how well read I am in other areas. Like my limited ability to engage in and grasp tech talk, a young student's ability to fully comprehend what she's reading is often limited by her lack of knowledge on a particular topic.

Our elementary schools would claim that, in fact, it's knowledge that they are teaching. They argue that by having students engage in discovery-based activities, projects and discussions, they are, in fact, conveying knowledge. More to the point, they are giving students the tools needed to acquire knowledge that is meaningful to them—the "learning to learn" principle.

The knowledge I'm talking about starts with facts and information—the kind of thing that is derided in our schools as "mere" facts. Facts are boring. Facts are disconnected. Yet I would contend that it's facts that allow not only students but also all individuals to understand context and meaning. How would we make any sense out of a story in the newspaper if we didn't know the facts? A large number of well-educated individuals know that there is conflict in the Middle East, particularly where Israel is involved, but they can't understand how it got to be that way and the reasons behind the conflict. The "mere" facts regarding the history of the region immediately allow us to understand and engage in more critical thinking about the matter. Facts and information are an important component of knowledge. Without them, our discussions are hollow and misinformed.

E. D. Hirsh, a critic of reading education in America and a proponent of knowledge-based education, states the matter bluntly: "To become a good comprehender, a child needs a great deal of knowledge."[47] He goes on to make this observation:

> While it's true that proficient reading and critical thinking are all-purpose abilities, they are not content-independent, formal skills at all but are always based on concrete, relevant knowledge and cannot be exercised apart from what psychologists call "domain-specific" knowledge. The only thing that transforms reading skills and critical thinking skills into general, all purpose abilities is a person's possession of general, all purpose knowledge.[48]

Like decoding, the acquiring of knowledge takes time. Unfortunately, as our schools move further from directly teaching knowledge, the more likely we will have students who have a limited grasp of what they're reading.

What Can Parents Do?

I've described reading education as a path that begins with decoding skills and leads to comprehension. Parents are sometimes inundated with advice from teachers and friends. But before you consider all of the advice, you must first understand where along the path to reading your child is.

Phonics

Before worrying about ensuring that your child is immersed in a literature-rich environment at home, examine her ability to decode language. If your child is a primary-elementary student (kindergarten to Grade 2), then the most logical place to begin is at the beginning with phonics. Even if your child is older than primary age, if she struggles with decoding, phonics is where you must begin.

When it comes to phonics, I often advise parents to seek out a resource or program that meets the following criteria:

- It should be incremental.
- It should allow for continual review.
- It should build upon prior concepts.

While it isn't a necessity, an easy-to-use assessment can also be beneficial, particularly for parents who really have no idea where to begin.

Incremental Learning

Since reading is not a natural process, it's vital that the steps to decoding are taught in small increments. This is of particular importance when we are working with primary-age children. The irony of the whole-language approach is that students tend to become overwhelmed, since they must learn hundreds of sight words and strategies for deciphering a word through context while, at the same time, being immersed and too often drowning in an environment rich in literature. It's simply too much all at once. By teaching phonics in small steps, we allow each lesson to be not only compact but also not easily forgotten.

Teaching phonics in small increments is also important for parents. From a practical point of view, Mom and Dad don't want to spend hours working with their very young son or daughter on phonics. Using incremental steps keeps the time short and productive, allowing the child to give her full attention and parents to avoid exasperation.

Continual Review

Review helps to solidify new information. While teaching phonics in incremental steps is productive, the benefits will quickly be lost if parents don't continually review what was learned. Review also allows a child to see the connections from one lesson to the next, and as each element builds, a child will begin to grasp the bigger picture. For example, with children who are new to letters, we begin with the alphabet. First, we ensure that a child knows each letter of the alphabet and the various sounds associated with each letter. From there, as we continue to review these steps, we combine or blend letters together. Slowly, surely, a child begins to understand the purpose of the alphabet and how letters can work together to form a word.

Review also helps parents. Don't be concerned that you may not remember phonics (if you were even taught phonics as a child). By reviewing with your child, you are also solidifying lessons in your own mind, and as you approach new lessons, you will see how everything is connected.

Building Upon Prior Lessons

Each new lesson should build upon the lesson before. If your child's understanding is to increase along with her ability, it's important that she sees how all of the lessons are stitched together. For example, if you were at the stage of teaching your child the consonant sounds of the alphabet, it would be pointless to jump to vowel sounds. While there is a connection between consonants and vowels, one does not directly build upon the other. Instead, we must first follow the path from letter sounds to letter combinations and, eventually, to what a vowel is and the sounds each vowel makes under what circumstance.

Helping Children Acquire Knowledge

While phonics offers an easy-to-follow path to teaching kids how to decode words, helping them acquire knowledge that leads to greater comprehension is not such a direct and simple road. Knowledge is acquired in many ways and, since this is the case, must be multifaceted. Of course, the pressing question when we talk about knowledge is: What kind of knowledge should our kids be acquiring? The simple answer is, as much as possible in as many subject areas as possible. How? I've observed three attributes in families where children have the knowledge to comprehend a wide-range of texts: parental interest, variety of topics and variety of modes.

Attribute #1: Parental Interest

It's no surprise that young children typically have (or pretend to have) the same interests as their parents. I love baseball, and even though many of my son's friends would rather watch paint dry than watch a game on television, my son also likes baseball. There are no other people in his life besides me who have an interest in the game, so naturally it's my interest in the game that my son has adopted as his own.

When we show a general level of curiosity in a number of things—whether current affairs, sports, the environment, history or other topics—two things occur with regard to our kids. First, they are exposed to information and facts they might not otherwise have access to. Second, they develop an interest in at least some, if not all, of the things that we as parents are curious about. Parents who show little interest in a wider range of things tend to have kids whose interests are limited. There are certainly children who buck this trend, but as a general rule, this is what happens.

Variety of Topics

In order for students to gain knowledge in a variety of areas, it makes sense to expose them to a variety of topics. The more a child is given the opportunity to learn about events in history, great works in art and literature, discoveries and advancements in science, the logic of math and current events, the greater the scope of her knowledge. The goal isn't for your son or daughter to become an expert in all of these areas, but for him or her to gain exposure, understanding and experience.

The acquisition of knowledge for increasing reading comprehension is well illustrated by a recent conversation I had with a friend. His daughter was reading the novel *The Hiding Place*. It's the story of Corrie ten Boom, a woman who lived in Holland during the Second World War when it was occupied by Germany. The story recounts her family's attempts to hide local Jews from the Germans. My friend explained to me that his daughter had trouble fully understanding the events she was reading about. Her understanding had little to do with her ability to read but with her lack of knowledge of World War II and, more specifically, the plight of the Jews in Nazi-occupied Holland.

Variety of Modes

The great thing about exposing your child to all of these topics and a host of others is that it can be done in many different ways—

making use of documentaries, museums, books, magazines, educational software, relevant websites, history and nature channels and pretty much any other forum where interesting facts, figures and stories are shared. While there is some debate in educational circles regarding what is most important for children to learn about, particularly in light of a global economy and ever-advancing technology, we shouldn't limit the kinds of facts, information and topics we expose them to.

Teaching your child to read is a process that requires time, patience and a logical process. Hirsch describes the process of reading education succinctly: "Becoming a skilled reader—a skilled user of language—is not fast or easy."[49] To many parents, the idea of helping children acquire the decoding and comprehension skills necessary to make them effective readers may seem daunting without the right strategy. Many schools are moving away from a strict adherence to a whole-language approach but hesitate to embrace the systematic teaching of phonics. While there are positive developments, they don't go far enough. The good news is that parents, with consistent but relatively short amounts of time, can impart the decoding skills their children need to read fluently and, later, with comprehension.

Our children can't gain knowledge without the interest and exposure that we, as parents, can provide for them. Fortunately, our children's opportunity to learn about a great variety of topics is only limited by the time and experiences we give them. In North America today, kids have more access to information through a wider variety of forums then ever before. All that's required is our own guidance, interest and time.

CHAPTER 8

The Skill of Learning

THERE ARE MANY STUDENTS WHO struggle in elementary and, later, in high school because they simply don't have good study and organizational skills, nor do they adopt the routines, habits and tools they need to succeed in school. So many perfectly capable and extremely bright young students short-change themselves because they aren't organized and lack preparation. The irony is that a lot of these very intelligent children end up believing that they're not very smart at all.

I've met many parents who, upon learning that their child isn't that organized or prepared, brush it off as being too simple an answer. After all, how much can organizational and study skills (or a lack of) affect learning? A lot, actually. Without them, time is poorly utilized, assignments are typically rushed or late, studying is crammed if it happens at all and an atmosphere of chaos and stress ensues. Not only does this affect the quality of work being done and the timeliness with which it's completed, but a lack of organizational and study skills only serves to take away from real learning. If a child's time isn't prioritized and organized, there will inevitably be little, if any, time to practice and master foundational skills in the core subject areas.

Many parents also assume that study and organizational skills are taught in school. Unfortunately, this simply isn't the case. While teachers will give reminders, tips and suggestions to students and parents regarding preparation and organization, these learning skills aren't taught deeply or consistently enough. Our schools seem to believe that giving occasional practical information on how to stay organized will lead to improved habits and routines. Organization and study preparation are skills, and like any skill, they need to be taught and then practiced over time with ongoing support. What does this all mean? It's up to the parents not only to ensure that their child is given the right information on how to stay organized and study, but also to teach their child how to put this information into practice.

Tools of the Trade

While having effective and simple routines plays an important role in your child's ability to work in an organized and efficient manner, having the right tools is also vital. A major problem among struggling students is their ignorance of, or inability to use, the essential tools of learning. One of the reasons we assume that schools actually teach children how to organize and prioritize is that many schools do provide some tools. The most obvious example of this is the day planner. Many elementary schools across North America provide each student with a planner. A lot of teachers, particularly those who teach in elementary and middle schools, require their students to utilize the planners by recording due dates and homework requirements. Some of them expect students to have the planner signed by the parents. The reality is that, over the course of the school year, these habits and expectations often fall by the wayside. Planners can be very useful tools, but unfortunately, many students never come to truly understand and appreciate their value.

Whether it's a planner, electronic organizer, calendar, computer or some other useful tool for organization, teach your child how organizational tools can be used to make her academic life easier. This is of particular importance if you're attempting to work with your child on certain school-related habits and routines, since the application of these tools will require regular use. But don't stop with showing your child how to use a tool—constantly monitor its use and offer guidance each step of the way.

While a day planner can be an extremely useful tool for your child, there is more to helping your child become organized. Parents should take stock of every aspect of their child's daily life. It can be a useful exercise for both the student and the parents to sit and make a checklist of organizational needs. This would begin with an overview of your child's day, starting from the time she gets up to time spent in school to time after school. Take a closer look at those circumstances where your child experiences stress, frustration and pressure. Does it appear as though any or all of the situations are a result of some form of disorderliness? For example, some students rush out the door for school in the morning, dishevelled and dazed after attempting to finish leftover homework. Hurriedly they get their things together and dash off to catch their bus. Others describe a sense of dread when they arrive in class and come to the realization that some homework assignment was forgotten or they are completely unprepared for a quiz or test. This exercise gives parents a proper perspective on their child's day and helps bring to light their child's organizational needs.

Next, think about which tools would be useful to help your child with her organizational needs. These tools should be practical and within easy reach. While a planner may seem like an obvious choice, there are some things to consider: Should your child's planner have space for reminder notes? Is there enough room to write assignments and due dates? Is the planner made of sturdy and abuse-resistant material? Is it easy to carry in a backpack? Some students may find a handheld PDA, smartphone or tablet attractive, but is it practical? Paper-based planners are considerably less expensive and typically quicker to use. In addition, electronic devices like smartphones contain a lot more than just organizers—including games, music and Wi-Fi—that are sure to be a much bigger draw than the organizer itself. However, if it motivates a student to remain organized, then an appropriate electronic device could be a great fit. Here are other useful organizational tools to consider:

- *Digital Clock*—Many students don't have a bedside clock, and each morning can start off much more smoothly if a student determines to get up with enough time to dress, eat, review any school material and be off to school without being caught in a rush.

- *Whiteboard*— Sticky notes or notes written on scrap paper often become lost or forgotten. A whiteboard, especially if hung or set in a place where it can't be missed, is easily accessible, easily revised and easily seen.

- *Wall Calendar*—While it's expected that a student should keep an up-to-date planner, a wall calendar can serve as great backup. It also keeps track of personal and social events your child may not include in her planner, such as family events, practices and vacations. Wall calendars come in the form of dry-erase whiteboards or paper-based tear sheets. Like the whiteboard, a wall calendar should be placed where it's easily visible. With my daughter, considering her unique schedule, we found it very useful to put long-term or repeating school deadlines on a wall calendar as well, such as projects, weekly homework, and regular tests. It can be difficult to keep track of things like this on a planner since, with a planner, you typically only view a week at a time.

- *Portable Filer*—For keeping track of papers, preventing loss or damage to assignments and ensuring that assignments are handed in on time, portable filers are excellent tools. Since there are a variety of portable filers, parents should make sure the one their child chooses is durable. Cardboard-based filers tend to fall apart long before the end of the school year. Filers should also have several dividers with ample space. Finally, a portable filer should be lightweight and, as the name suggests, portable. A filer can be divided into sections, such as subjects and completed assignments to be handed in.

Parents should never make the assumption that their child will know precisely how to use various organizational tools. While the goal is to have your child eventually use these tools consistently, monitor your child and keep her accountable. As she begins to use them effectively, she'll need less and less reminding. However, never get to the point where there's no more oversight. Kids, being human, can slip back into old habits. Even the most diligent students can use some checking in from time to time.

Marc Lapointe

Organizing Space

An organized and regular space can go a long way in helping a student maximize homework and study time. I encounter a lot of students who don't have a study space and typically do their homework in environments that are full of distractions, like in front of the television or in a high traffic area. Many parents are so grateful that their child is doing any homework at all that they shy away from making a distraction-free and organized space an issue. However, I have consistently observed the difference in the quality of work when a student studies where there are distractions and where there are very few. Having an organized space has numerous benefits:

- There a very few things that are an immediate distraction. In other words, there are no sights or sounds that can easily draw a student's attention from his or her work.

- There is less "wandering," since materials are close at hand. Do you have a son or daughter who seems to waste time simply looking for materials like pens, pencils or paper? Having everything in one organized space means it's easily accessible and a student always knows where to find what she needs.

- There is less likelihood of schoolwork and materials going missing. When a student parks herself in random locations around the house, that's when things have a greater tendency to get lost. When there's a regular workspace where all materials are close at hand, a student knows to automatically go to that space if any schoolwork goes missing.

Some students prefer to work in a central area of the home, such as the kitchen. I often suggest that, instead of the kitchen, parents create a space near the kitchen that allows for optimal organization and storage of materials and freedom of distractions. Bedrooms typically make for the best balance since they're off the beaten path of regular household traffic and therefore free of regular distractions. As a bonus, your child can add more personal touches that add to her comfort.

Study spaces shouldn't include access to televisions or phones. I'm of the opinion that they should also be free of a computer. I realize some parents would argue that a computer is an essential tool for research, presentations and essay writing. Time and again, however, a computer proves itself to be more of a hindrance, since students can wander the Internet and e-mail or instant message their friends. My suggestion to families is to have a separate area for the computer. Before using the computer for school-related projects that include research, writing or presentations, a student should be prepared to make the time efficient and focused. Too often a student may sit behind a computer with very little idea where to begin. When it comes to research, your child should know what topic she wishes to read more about. If, for example, a child must put together a project on a specific animal like an eagle, it is an inefficient use of computer time to allow the child to type "eagle" in the Internet search. This leads to time wasted browsing various websites with little direction. Instead, your child should come to the computer with a list of specific questions or topics related to the eagle. This will narrow the search terms and allow for better use of the computer and the Internet in particular.

An organized workspace should include a plentiful supply

of paper—both lined and blank—as well as writing utensils, sharpeners, erasers, a stapler, a three-hole punch, a wastebasket and, above all, space. A desk with ample surface space is essential. In addition, drawers and shelves complement an organized workspace. Drawers must be organized and each should have a specific function, such as a paper drawer or a pencil drawer. A wastebasket should always be nearby. Good lighting is very important, so a desk should include a lamp. A clock can also be useful, but be mindful that some students are prone to obsessive clock-watching and end up spending more time worrying about when their designated homework time will come to an end than focusing on the completion and quality of the work.

Depending on the type of space a student may be using, a whiteboard and wall calendar can prove very useful. Whiteboards are great for posting reminders, for top-of-mind information and even for brainstorming. Even though planners have calendars, a large visible wall calendar ensures that important dates are front and centre and, therefore, easily noticed.

While the most important consideration for a student's workspace should be functionality, aesthetics should not be completely ignored. Many people, including young students, seem to be more productive in environments that they perceive to be pleasant and comfortable. If possible, work with your child to put some thought into the looks of the workspace environment. With a bedroom workspace, there may be little need to create a more inviting area, but if the space is in another area of the house, such as a kitchen or den, you may want to get creative. This doesn't mean you must redecorate; it can be as simple as making a small corner of the room a little more personalized for the sake of your child.

The Art of Time Management

When we talk about time as it pertains to planning and organization, we're speaking specifically about a student's ability to properly judge how much time it will take to complete an assignment successfully. It isn't unusual for a student to misjudge how long it will take to finish homework, complete a project or prepare for a test. How often do kids tell their parents that the homework is "easy" and it'll take only a few minutes to complete? Parents may find out later that the homework was neither easy nor quick. The result is a stressed-out student who has waited until the last minute to finish the homework assignment. Between the rush to complete the work, mental fatigue and a lack of motivation because the task turned out to be much harder than expected, little has occurred in the way of reinforcement or quality work—assuming the work was finished at all.

The first key lesson in the area of organization that parents should teach their children is proper time management. I believe that this concept can be conveyed to children even at an early age. While a child in the primary grades may not have much need to manage time for homework or test preparation, she can certainly benefit from learning the concept of prioritizing. For example, many parents struggle to some extent with teaching young children to clean up their messes. Things like toys and colouring books are often left spread out around the kitchen table, the family-room floor, the stairway or the child's bedroom. Here is where a lesson in time management can begin. A child can be told that, until these items are put back in their proper places, there will be no time for other, more fun activities. Consistency and diligence are the key for the parent. There may be complaining and protesting. The disorganization may even continue for some time, but parents must remain firm in their expectations.

In the beginning, it would be prudent for a parent to offer some help in order to demonstrate how the clean-up should be done. Help doesn't mean that a parent does it all. After some time, it's not unreasonable to expect that your child can perform the clean-up entirely on her own. Once the task is completed, your son or daughter will be free to play, go outside or do whatever he or she was planning on doing.

Whether it involves cleaning up toys or making the bed, these simple early lessons demonstrate the value of time management. If a child can learn that certain chores or responsibilities must be attended to first, she'll appreciate the value of having free time that's nag-free and guilt-free. Children will need occasional reminding, but that isn't a sign of failure on the part of the parents. If a child responds quickly and without complaint to a mother or father's gentle reminder, then a parent can be encouraged that the child is beginning to learn the concept of time management.

As a young student advances through school, time management becomes more critical. Extracurricular activities, such as sports, music and friends, all begin to compete for her attention. In addition to these increasing interests, there are more homework assignments, projects, papers, tests and exams to complete and prepare for. Many of the students I work with who struggle in school at one level or another lack the ability to manage time effectively. Their struggles have very little to do with how capable they are but have much more to do with the fact that they haven't been taught how to properly manage their time and set priorities. I have often listened to panic-stricken parents who can find no rhyme or reason in their children's academic struggles. In other cases, the parents will tell me that their son or daughter is lazy and wastes time watching television, playing on the computer or hanging out with friends. In either case, our attention, of necessity, shifts away from the specific subjects the student is struggling with and focuses on organization. Once I'm able to convince the parents that this is where the problem lies and that our efforts should be on teaching time-management concepts, the progress we make is remarkable.

Homework and test preparation must always take precedence. That's the attitude parents must have and children must understand. All other activities, including sports, must be secondary. This doesn't mean that other important pursuits and interests must be neglected. On the contrary, students who are heavily involved in activities like sports teams are, on average, more successful students. The reason for this is their ability to prioritize their time and follow through on their efforts. I can think of no better example than my daughter. At the age of 13, she's involved in competitive gymnastics. She must train 25 hours each week. This of course means that she misses some school and has even less time to complete homework. She is a successful student and near the top of her class with regard to grades. Does this mean that she is somehow gifted intellectually? While my daughter is bright, her academic success comes from her ability to prioritize and organize her time. Was she born with the ability to manage her time and recognize its value? Of course not, but my wife has been very purposeful in ensuring that she learns about time management.

While my daughter serves as a personal example, there are countless students who dedicate a good deal of time to sports, music or various clubs and organizations. Many of these students are strong academically. They have learned to prioritize what is most important and manage their time in order to meet their goals and obligations.

I encourage parents to always look for opportunities to demonstrate how time management has made an impact. If a child prepared for a test and did relatively well, encourage her and show her how, by being prepared, she was able to achieve a good grade. If a student completes a project or assignment well before the due date and suddenly has much more free time to enjoy, parents should point out that working ahead not only brought about some welcome free time but took away any stress associated with last-minute panic.

Teach Your Child to Organize Time for Homework

One of the greatest challenges for some students is effectively estimating the length of time it will take to complete a homework assignment or project. It seems that, more often than not, students underestimate how much time they'll need. This inevitably leads to late nights, frantic mornings and an overall greater level of stress for both student and parents.

Even though you and your child may have prioritized the work, it's just as important to quickly examine the expected length of time for the homework to be completed in. I encourage parents to first ask their son or daughter how long a particular assignment may take. For example, if your child is responsible for completing 10 math questions, what does she feel is a reasonable amount of time to finish the work? The goal isn't to rush your child or to enforce strict time limits, but to have your child think in more detail about the process. If she states that it will probably take an hour to finish the 10 questions, ask why it will take that long. You'll often discover that she may be struggling to understand a concept or is slow on the procedures or may simply be trying to manipulate the time to avoid too much work. Whatever the reason, you'll be better armed to provide practical help for your child. If it appears that the work will take a little longer than expected to complete, help your child schedule appropriate breaks. If it seems that it won't take long at all, work with your child on filling the remainder of the time with activities that have value, such as reading or review.

Perhaps the single biggest reason students underestimate how long it may take to complete an assignment is a lack of attention to detail. There are, of course, many people who have the big picture in mind but neglect to consider all of the small steps it will take to reach that goal. As adults, when it comes to our careers, we often have the assistance of others to help us achieve the end result. In the workplace, there are those who have vision and leadership but are supported by colleagues who have a special talent for attending to the details. Unfortunately for our kids, they're on their own when it comes to not only completing a homework assignment or project but also doing it well.

Teach Your Child to Organize Time for Projects

When it comes to larger projects, a student must take the time to not only consider but also plan the way forward. Parents can be a huge help in this area, since Mom or Dad can go through a checklist of things to plan for:

- *Confirm the due date for the project.* It's important to keep this at the forefront of any planning and then to work from there. A great habit for students to adopt is to plan to complete their project at least one day before the due date. In the minds of many students, this may seem counterproductive. However, as with many endeavours, some unexpected delays or changes to a project might occur. Imposing a due date before the teacher's due date allows for a cushion.

- *What is the "big idea"?* Having a big idea or

imaginative thought can be a great motivator, so start with what your child envisions as the final product.

- *What are the requirements for the project?* Sometimes students generate impressive ideas that focus more on the appearance of the final project than on the academic requirements. This is typical with the average elementary-school science-fair project, where a student may be motivated to display some "cool" visual but totally ignores the whole purpose of the project. While unique displays may impress the average observer, these projects suffer on an academic level.

- *What resources and materials are needed?* A student should write down what she needs, from research notes to construction material (if applicable). Sometimes the type of material needed will prove to be too impractical, and this will require a change of plans. It's better for your child to come to this realization early in her project than when she's invested time and energy. This is also where a student has the flexibility to either make alterations or change her idea altogether.

- *What are the timelines?* This is where a student must get into the finer details of project planning. There should be set dates by which certain aspects of the project must be completed. Research, rough drafts, final drafts, materials and any construction should all be carefully planned in order to meet the self-imposed deadline.

Teach Your Child to Organize Time for Test Preparation

While the principles I've described above apply to the successful completion of projects, the general philosophy can also be applied to test preparation. Even when studying, students benefit greatly from preparing well before the scheduled test day. Some students may claim that cramming the night before is the best way for them to study, but it isn't an advisable approach to test preparation. For students who generally have poor test results, the root of the problem can usually be traced back to preparation. I've met a lot of parents who claim that their child does study but seems to have a mental block or becomes very anxious. In many of these cases, a noticeable cycle evolves. A student will study, but usually the night before. Since time is limited and the average person tends to lose focus after only 45 minutes of studying, a student will spend most of her time reviewing material that she already understands. Also, since she's probably pressed for time, little practice or reinforcement takes place. By the next day, a student may not feel all that confident, since her grasp of a host of concepts and procedures is shaky at best. The result is usually a poor test score.

Like projects, studying can be carefully planned. The number-one reason why many students refuse to study for an upcoming test several days before is the unfounded belief that they would have to devote hours of study time each day in order to prepare. This notion is often based on an assumption that studying is a marathon session taking several hours. Planning for studying involves three main components:

1. Reviewing, practicing and reinforcing the most difficult concepts first;
2. Reviewing easier concepts later; and

3. A light study session the night before.

The further from the test date a student begins her preparations, the less time required for each study session. The reason a child must spend hours cramming is because there's so much material to cover. When a student begins the process of studying for a specific test several days to a week before, each study session need not be any longer than 20 to 30 minutes in length.

It's imperative that, when you and your child plan study sessions, the concepts that are most difficult for your child are given primary focus. It's common sense for a student to spend much of her study time on material she still has difficulty with, but so often, struggling students instead spend their time looking over material that they feel most comfortable with. That's why cramming is so counterproductive. If a student can't master each challenging concept or piece of information the night before (and it usually doesn't happen), then she no longer has the luxury of seeking academic help and reviewing further the next day. When it comes time to write the test, it's too late. I advise parents to never buy into their children's argument that cramming works best since most of the information won't escape their memory between studying and test taking.

It can be deeply frustrating as an educator to see the number of students who continually struggle in school because they don't have the ability to get properly organized. No, it isn't a "silver bullet" that will remedy every academic challenge that your child may be facing, but it can still have a profound affect on your son or daughter's success and, to be frank, we are only disadvantaging our kids if we choose to ignore its importance. The challenge for us as parents, then, is to teach our children how to be organized, how to use the right tools that will help them and how to keep using strategies that work. No matter how much we might hope and believe that learning skills can somehow be picked up and put into practice by our kids over time, this makes little sense. To put it simply: It won't happen without our intervention.

Chapter 9

The Habits and Routines of Successful Students

THERE ARE TWO HALVES TO study and organizational skills. While I've taken the opportunity to discuss the latter in the previous chapter, we can't forget that studying is also an important skill. While study skills involve the actual preparation for tests and exams, they're also about a student's learning preparation. While a student might study for a specific test, study skills really involve the method of working in a daily manner that allows for continued and meaningful learning. With the proper study skills, actual test preparation is made so much easier because a student doesn't have to cram but, instead, reviews material and information she is already familiar with.

Study skills are also about working efficiently and productively—whether it involves homework completion, some kind of project or assignment or getting ready for a test. If you're confounded by your child's lack of academic productivity, you're not alone. It might seem like your child is keeping busy whenever she does her homework or studies for a test, but her grades and test results don't seem to reflect her apparent hard work. Quite often, however, what appears to be busy and productive study time is really just busywork and time wasting. Even your child might feel as though she's working hard but, in reality, her time isn't being used efficiently on relevant tasks. Simply working hard isn't always enough. Study skills allow a student to work in a way that doesn't waste her effort and hard work.

The Right Routines

Many aspects of our lives have established routines. While not everything needs to be based on some kind of orderly schedule, routines allow us to have a certain level of comfort and security when it comes to various tasks and responsibilities. This is especially true for children. The problem is that, while many kids benefit from routine, they often don't have the knowledge, experience and discipline to begin and stick with routines that will help them academically. One of the simplest but most effective ways to establish a beneficial routine with your child when it comes to schoolwork is through a daily standard of previewing, reviewing and following up.

Previewing

Previewing is as straightforward as it sounds. Before each homework or study session, you and your child take a few minutes to preview what she should be working on. Previewing has several benefits: It keeps you as the parent in the loop and keeps unpleasant surprises to a minimum; it helps your child to prioritize the work (and since prioritizing is one of the characteristics of self-sufficiency, this is a great opportunity to teach and model how to focus on the most important things first); and it helps you as the parent to anticipate any help your child may need.

Through the process of previewing, we can help our children learn several important things:

- *There is a difference between being busy and actually accomplishing something meaningful.* This can be done by first asking your child what aspects of an assignment should be given most of her attention and why. As a parent, you can give direction with regard to what needs the most attention.

- *Successfully completing an assignment doesn't have to take a great deal of time.* It's ironic that many students hate homework because it's time-consuming and then spend much of their homework time being unproductive, thereby increasing the length of time it takes to finish homework.

- *Previewing is preparation for learning.* When a child understands what is expected, what type of information is important and relevant and what tools she'll need to accomplish her task, she starts work in the right frame of mind.

Reviewing

Just as important as previewing homework or assignments with our children is reviewing the work. This process helps to reinforce expectations and outcomes. Numerous students will rush through their homework in order to get it over and done with. Many parents, in turn, will allow themselves to feel satisfied that the homework was completed. Inevitably, assignments come home with a poor grade or incomplete—and on top of that, since the sole goal for the student was to finish the homework and not to learn from reinforcement, there is a spill over effect into test preparation.

Reviewing homework can go a long way in ensuring that assignments are not only completed but also meet or exceed expectations. In order for our children to become successful in their academics, we must help them understand the connection between the quality of their work and the grades they'll receive. This is part of moving past immediate gratification. When a child simply gets homework done and out of the way, there is an immediate but very short-lived payoff: free time. However, ask almost any parent if the bit of free time earned was worth it when the child receives a mediocre grade, and you'll likely hear a resounding *no*. By reviewing academic work with your child, you not only work toward ensuring greater quality in your child's work, but you can also help her start making the connection between effort and result.

Follow-Up

Our work as parents doesn't end with reviewing homework. There should always be follow-up. This can range from simply asking how your child did on a quiz or assignment to examining a graded test or project. Follow-up is an imperative element in the parents' quest to help their child understand that quality effort will ultimately result in quality grades. A student should always assume that, whatever the outcome of an assignment or test, her parents will want to know the result. Sometimes this provides motivation, since it's an extra measure of accountability. It also keeps parents in the loop. I'm always surprised when parents share with me their utter shock when they saw their child's report card and discovered just how poorly she was doing in school. Parents who follow-up with their child are never outright surprised by a report card.

While previewing, reviewing and follow-up are all parent-initiated routines; the ultimate goal is to bring your child to the point where it becomes a student-initiated routine. This doesn't mean that parents will have the freedom to shrug off their involvement, but that there will be less need for reminders and initiation. Eventually, a student will come to see these routines as invaluable and will seek her parents' input and involvement.

Organizing and Remembering Important Information

I consult regularly with parents who describe their child as unable to recall information or memorize facts, formulas and concepts. While some are firmly convinced that there is some learning disability involved, the truth is that learning disabilities are much more rare than we think. Yet even for those students who have a diagnosed learning disability, educators are prone to water down their expectations. In the long run, all students, regardless of learning disabilities, must develop a strategy for organizing and remembering information. Unfortunately, many teachers, parents and students look for a "silver bullet" for remembering information. While for some remembering things comes relatively easy, the reality for the rest of us is that there is no quick and easy method. The ability to remember information, particularly at an academic level, requires consistent review and repetition.

Review, Repeat, Review

Recall and memorization are not just about having the ability to hear or see a piece of information and lock it into the brain. If we were to conduct a survey, I'm sure that the majority of individuals would say that this kind of retention just doesn't happen for them (myself included). Most of us remember things that, having some meaning, become repetitious and routine, or we have spent time practicing. Unfortunately, many parents fail to consider these basic concepts regarding their child's own difficulties with remembering.

Students are often reluctant to follow any advice that involves repetitive work. In the eyes of a child, it can seem monotonous and not terribly interesting. In addition, some parents may not have very favourable attitudes toward repetition simply because it's viewed as a traditional, and therefore out-dated, approach to understanding and mastering a new concept. But repetition is not just about saying something over and over until it has been committed to memory. It involves the practice of review and reinforcement.

Countless students fail to recognize that learning and success in school have a lot to do with being proactive. When a student is proactive, she routinely reviews material at the end of the school day and, if needed, completes practice questions—even if they haven't been assigned. This strategy works particularly well for students who struggle with memorizing or remembering facts and formulas. It can also reduce the time dedicated to test preparation and minimizes stress and anxiety. Since the student has already reviewed and practiced, sometimes several times for a single concept or lesson, there is very little to prepare for whenever there is a test. Surprise quizzes, a favourite with some teachers, are rarely a problem for the student who has already reviewed and practiced.

This type of routine, admittedly, is a difficult one to begin. In some households where the homework load seems insurmountable, the idea of engaging in daily review is met with considerable opposition by both the parents and the student. However, homework assignments can be part of the review and practice process. Before your child begins any assignment, have her spend time reviewing material from the day's lesson and then approach the homework as an opportunity to practice and reinforce what was reviewed. Daily review time need not take longer than 20 minutes and can require as little as 10 minutes depending on the amount of material to review and how challenging a concept is to a child.

It is no coincidence that, particularly in math, children who practice basic concepts using flash cards, quick and easy worksheets or computer programs typically experience greater success in school. Repetition is a valuable tool for ensuring that your child overcomes the memory challenge. Some would argue that flash cards and other tools for memorization help very little. The problem in many cases is that parents don't engage their son or daughter in these activities on a regular basis; in these circumstances, there's little benefit. Repetition works only if it is, well, *repeated*, at least several times throughout each week.

Sorting Through the Information

Not too long ago, my son handed me a magazine article and asked me to read it. The article was written specifically for children with a Grade 4 to 6 reading ability. Within 30 seconds, I had scanned its contents, and to the amazement of my young son, I was able to recall its most interesting facts. My son thought I was some kind of speed-reader. I told him that I had skim-read the article, which meant that I didn't read every word but, instead, quickly sorted through to find the most relevant information. Given my experience attending university for undergraduate and graduate programs, teaching and running a business, I have learned to sort through written information to find the most interesting or important facts.

For many students who struggle with remembering important facts and concepts, one of the biggest challenges is sorting through written information. My son, who was impressed with how fast I had reviewed the magazine article, didn't yet have the ability to identify relevant information quickly and effectively. He, like many students his age, always read every word in the textbook in an attempt to harvest every tidbit of information. While this process can be somewhat time-consuming, many students will eventually be able to pick out the important facts and retain them. For other students, words, sentences and paragraphs are a confusing mass.

Parents shouldn't assume their child will be able to naturally sort through a textbook or article, identify the important facts and retain them. For some students, the problem begins with simple boredom. With others, particularly young students, there is a greater focus on speed than on comprehension. Whatever the cause, as parents begin to teach their child how to sort through written information, they should begin with identifying what to look for. This can happen in several ways, depending on the desired outcome. To begin, teach your children to follow a simple checklist:

- *What is the title or subtitle?* Sometimes children will overlook something that appears obvious and simple. The title itself can tell the student what she can expect to read about.

- *What information is contained in the introductory and concluding paragraph?* The first paragraph of a chapter or article can tell the reader a lot about what kind of information can be found in the rest of the reading.

- *What is shared in the topic sentence of each new paragraph?* At times children can get bogged down in the wordiness of a paragraph and be unable to understand or describe its content. The first sentence of a paragraph usually contains a synopsis of its content.

These simple steps may not necessarily fix a child's comprehension problems, but they allow a student to approach reading in a methodical and organized manner. When kids see a page filled with words and focus on what looks like a massive jumble of information that can only be teased out through agonizing hours of concentration, having an organized approach helps them to clear the biggest hurdle. As a child begins to glean information, whether it's for reading comprehension assignments or for projects that require a summary of the information, she will begin to grow more confident.

Teaching your child to skim for information requires careful guidance. While it can be taught to younger children, it is most appropriate for students in the higher elementary grades. It's a process that takes time, so parents should not feel discouraged if, after only a few sittings, their son or daughter still seems frustrated and slow. As you begin, have your child read the first sentence of each paragraph in a chapter or article and don't allow her to go further. Based on those few sentences, have your child describe what the reading is about as well as the main point of each paragraph.

When your child begins to master this concept, the next step is to locate specific pieces of information within the body of the reading. At this point, a student should be able to recognize that the introductory sentence of a paragraph will give definite clues to the information it contains. For example, if a child must answer a comprehension question that asks about the main industry in the province of British Columbia, Canada, she would scan for paragraphs that have an introductory sentence that contains key ideas like "British Columbia" and "industry." After some time and practice, a student will learn that, in order to find the answers to comprehension questions, she need not reread the entire chapter.

The process of skim-reading should mark the beginning of building a student's confidence in reading. When a page stuffed with sentences and paragraphs no longer intimidates a child but, instead, she recognizes them as an orderly method of communicating information, then she'll feel at greater ease reading the entire chapter, article or book. The principles of previewing, reviewing and follow-up are essential in this process. Parents must also realize that it takes time, and so Mom and Dad must remain consistent and committed to the process.

While we have looked at a number of specific strategies for parents and students throughout this section, there are some very easy, practical yet effective tools for students who have difficulty organizing their thoughts or remembering crucial facts and concepts.

- *Brainstorming*: This is an idea that is constantly reinforced in the classroom, particularly in the elementary grades. Yet for many students who struggle with writing, it's often ignored (unless assigned by the teacher). A lot of hard-working students dive into the writing process without giving any detailed thought as to the organization of their paper or story. Brainstorming allows students to generate ideas from a single topic. It provides a visual of the organizational process in which a student can easily discard ideas in favour of better ones.

- *Mnemonics*: Here's another age-old method for remembering facts. The idea is to associate words or letters that can be remembered by the student with specific pieces of information. For young students, one example is directions on a map: Never Eat Soggy Wieners represents North, East, South and West.

- *Reading Aloud*: While some students might be uncomfortable reading aloud as they review a chapter in their textbook, it's remarkable how much more information can be retained. For some, silent reading allows for too many distractions, whether it's her own thoughts or outside noises. Reading aloud can dampen these distractions.

- *Breaking It Down*: This is a particularly useful tool for memorizing long lists or passages. All too often, young students will convince themselves that they must memorize an entire list of facts or a lengthy passage (such as a poem) in one sitting. Instead, break down the facts or passage into manageable pieces. These pieces can be organized according to order or topic. This allows a student to focus on the mastery of each piece and not worry about the whole. The concept of breaking it down also applies to writing and is an extension of brainstorming. In this case, a student splits the writing process into rough draft (paying no attention to neatness, grammar or spelling at this point), revision (this is where grammar and spelling get fixed), final draft for editing and neat final draft to be handed in.

Special attention should be given to each stage, and they should not be done in the same sitting.

- *Reading the Questions First*: Teachers often assign reading coupled with a series of comprehension questions to complete. Many students will attempt to complete the assignment in that order: read, then answer. However, by reading the questions first and then reading the text, a student has prepared her mind to identify the important facts. When the passage is read first, a student can lose concentration or forget much of what was read. By knowing what the questions are, a student can maintain a sharper focus.

- *Self-Testing*: This is an exercise that works best when a parent is present. Self-testing involves the student piecing together a series of quizzes and then completing them. In fact, a majority of students, particularly in middle and high school, find that when they quiz each other in preparation for a test, they are much more able to recall important facts. The challenge is in ensuring that the right questions are asked. Parents can help kids piece together the right questions by having them review homework assignments, summaries and notes.

This chapter is in no way a comprehensive guide to helping your child develop the habits and routines that lead to greater academic success. It does, however, emphasize the value of effective strategies and routines and the unquestionable need for parents to teach them. Teaching academic routines is only the beginning; in reality, it's a process that takes time and consistency.

There are a lot of programs and books available to parents that can be very helpful. Be warned, though: Any book or program that claims study habits and homework routines can be learned with little supervision and in a short period of time should be ignored. While it's tempting to believe that there are shortcuts to establishing the right routines, the reality is there are none that will allow your child to become an efficient, persistent, self-sufficient student.

CHAPTER 10

The Intangibles

SOCIAL JUSTICE, BULLYING AND TOLERANCE are all hot topics in North American society. Parents, educators, governments and almost anyone who pays attention are constantly wrestling with how we can effectively "love thy neighbour as thyself." Everyone has different ideas on how this can be done and what is most important to convey. My goal in this chapter isn't to delve into the complex and sometimes controversial details of including issues of social justice in the school curriculum. I will say, however, that regardless of how we may feel about the role of our schools in teaching kids about tolerance and acceptance, I do believe that there are character traits that lend themselves in a positive way toward academic success. I call these traits "intangibles" simply because, as the term implies, they're difficult to observe at a glance, difficult to actually teach and not always a guarantee of success in school or in life. Perhaps even more perplexing is that, sometimes, even the efforts of the most well-meaning and well-intentioned parents to raise their children to be "good kids" don't have the effect they hoped for. Still other kids, regardless of their circumstances, develop a positive attitude and outlook even though there seems to be no explanation for how this came about. My goal is to discuss how we might, as parents, give our kids the best possible chance of developing those intangibles, or character traits, that will best prepare them for success in school and beyond.

While my line of work consists mainly of helping young, struggling students achieve success in their academics, I also meet many children who are successful in their academics, have an enthusiasm for learning, are diligent and, overall, seem self-sufficient. What most of these kids possess are certain characteristics that have been developed and nurtured over time. Responsibility, effort, perseverance, wisdom and integrity—these intangibles are present, to some degree, in many successful students. Let me be clear: While these characteristics may evoke images of calm, peaceful and perfect children, that isn't my intention. We are, after all, talking about children. Even the most angelic kids will, at times, misbehave and frustrate their parents. However, as you'll see, academic success is not just about the right teaching approach or a student's level of preparation or organization, it's about the right attitude as well.

Throughout this book I have emphasized how important common sense is and how parents, through consistently helping in small ways, can lead their children to academic success. Some of this discussion has dealt with our society's focus on self-esteem and how it has hijacked our schools and interfered with real learning within the average classroom. Responsibility, effort, perseverance, wisdom and integrity—these are characteristics that aren't developed through a careful devotion to making our kids feel good about themselves. If you're a parent, as I am, you know that it's sometimes very tough to not give in to your kids. We don't want them to be irrevocably discouraged nor do we want them to think for one moment that we don't love them. That's why it's not easy for me to talk about the intangibles because, let's be honest, it takes time, patience and tough choices to ensure that our kids are truly people of positive character.

What Are the Intangibles?

It's one thing to say that traits like responsibility, effort and perseverance are good things for our kids to have, but since we're talking about kids, what do these intangibles mean and look like? I could easily write an entire book on the subject (and many have been written on it), but let's examine what I mean in a more straightforward manner.

Responsibility

Can anyone deny that, in order to be a successful student, a child must be responsible? While, as parents, we must have a direct hand in teaching and helping our kids to be responsible, the goal is to lead them to the point where they become wholly responsible for things like homework, test preparation and organization. Responsibility often involves doing something that one doesn't wish to do but must be done—and to the best of one's ability. Doesn't this describe what school is often like for our children? They will constantly be met with tasks that they see as anything but fun or interesting. If a student's response is to always hide from or shrug off schoolwork merely because it isn't interesting, then she will never learn self-sufficiency and delayed gratification, and she's unlikely to work for and earn better grades.

Students who learn to be responsible don't make excuses for their academic shortcomings. For example, on a regular basis, I hear students explain what a lousy teacher they have. The teacher, they insist, is to blame for their late assignments, since it was the teacher who didn't remind the students of due dates or homework. It's the teacher's fault that the student consistently failed quizzes and tests because the teacher didn't give enough advance warning. The teacher doesn't like the student. The teacher is too young. The teacher is too old. The list of excuses goes on and on. This isn't the attitude of a responsible student. Worse yet are the parents who, instead of challenging their child's excuses, easily accept them and, without ever having spoken with the teacher, make strong assumptions about that person. Responsibility is about taking ownership and, regardless of the challenges, looking for a way to succeed.

Organization, attentiveness, participation and preparation are skills that responsible students must work toward. For the most part, they don't just come naturally. Students who have been taught to be responsible have a desire to succeed. In order to do so, they adopt and practice skill sets that will help them accomplish this goal. A responsible student doesn't need to be constantly reminded by her parents to complete homework, study for tests or get organized. Responsibility doesn't mean that parents are never needed to help children with homework, just that a student doesn't rely on her parents to do the work for her and, ultimately, gains a good deal of satisfaction from accomplishing a homework assignment by her own effort.

Effort

I recently perused a book on achieving personal wealth. The author's premise was that becoming wealthy was easy and, in reality, took very little effort. Throughout the book, the author described many examples of individuals who bought and sold real estate with little or no money down or engaged in some other get-rich-quick scheme that he endorsed. I can't say from personal experience if any of the advice found in that book actually worked, since I eventually regarded it as pure fantasy. Most wealthy individuals I know or have met tell me about the amount of hard work and effort it took to become that way. Not only did it involve hard work, it often meant that they experienced failure once, twice or even more along the way. My point is that, if an individual wishes to become successful in any endeavour, it will likely involve a good deal of effort. Similarly, effort usually runs hand-in-hand with academic success.

Many parents will tell me that their son or daughter does work hard in school and has little to show for it. It's tough to explain to these parents that effort does not always result in an immediate pay-off. Just like many successful and wealthy business people, students can have a fair share of setbacks and failures along the way. Effort involves more than just one Herculean push. It is about resilience, determination and patience. If a child struggles in school, working harder also means getting the right help, staying organized, preparing, reviewing, practicing and even building positive relationships with teachers. For some students, this becomes a way of life, but in the end they reap the rewards.

Great intelligence doesn't always equal great success, even in school. This is a concept that many people struggle with. If you're smart, many believe, school should be easy. The reality is that there are many kids who are extremely intelligent but can barely pass their grade or subjects. The reason? There's no effort. I have talked with individuals who never regarded themselves as being particularly smart but were successful in their field. In almost every case, these people would shake their heads at the sheer waste of great intelligence in men and women who don't work hard. To them, hard work was the key to their success, while intelligence was merely a nice bonus. When a college graduate enters the workforce, grades may be important to some potential employers. Once a student is hired, though, their grades become a thing of the past and they are judged, among other things, by how hard they work.

Scores of parents share with me that one of their greatest desires for their child is for him or her to be a more motivated student. When students give their best effort in school, the positive results will lead to a greater sense of purpose. One of the by-products of purpose is excellence. When students strive for excellence, they come full circle to effort. Since excellence demands more than just the minimum required, the only solution is to put forth a greater effort.

Perseverance

There is a very close relationship between effort and perseverance. After all, in order to persevere—to keep trying—one must be making an effort in the first place. Perseverance doesn't set short time limits. It is about pushing forward even when circumstances become difficult. It's a mindset that refuses to accept failure as the final outcome. That isn't to say that failure never comes, but it doesn't have to represent the end.

Whenever I meet with a family, I often speak directly to the student about grades, school and the kind of help I can provide. I make it my mission to be honest with students about the fact that, if they want to improve in school with our help, they're going to have to persevere. I go on to tell them they will have to push past feelings of not being smart enough to get better grades. They'll have to adopt certain routines and habits that, at first, will feel like work. They may not even see great results in the short term. But if they persevere, the results will come. More often than not, these students respond with some enthusiasm—not because they're thrilled with the idea that there will be work involved, but because someone was straight with them about what it would take.

In today's world, we are bombarded with ads that preach the joys of instant gratification. Even many learning centres or educational programs are guilty of perpetuating this misleading message. They suggest that, by registering for their programs, a struggling child can instantly gain self-confidence, better grades and even a happier relationship with her parents. But what happens when a student doesn't experience success or even progress as immediately as she was led to believe? In many cases, that student will give up. If she can't become a better student after working through a program that works so well for others, then what hope is there? I have seen this response many times. Even the parents are ready to give up. A child who is taught to persevere doesn't surrender after setbacks. A child who perseveres will ultimately become a successful student.

Two by-products of perseverance are self-control and willpower. In order to achieve academic success, there are times when a student must have the willpower to avoid falling into habits, like procrastination, that can work against her. Self-control aids a student in the effort to become better organized, since at first glance, the tasks involved in becoming and remaining organized can seem daunting. There are moments when it seems as though there are more interesting things to do, but self-control helps the student put aside those feelings in order to accomplish the task at hand.

Fortitude

Fortitude is a characteristic we don't often think of when describing character and children, particularly in the realm of academics. At first glance, some may see it as synonymous with perseverance. It's true that fortitude and perseverance have similarities, but where perseverance involves patience when success doesn't come when hoped for or expected, fortitude describes the mental and emotional strength it takes to overcome adversity and difficulties of any kind.

For students, school is filled with challenges. For children in kindergarten, these challenges range from adjusting to time away from home and getting used to new routines. For the student in Grade 12, it involves final exams and acceptance into college or university. Throughout all the years of a student's life, she will struggle with increasing expectations, more demanding schedules, homework, tests, exams, projects, peers, teachers and the list goes on. In order to navigate through the challenges and obstacles that school inevitably presents, young people must have the determination and drive to not only be successful as students but also grow positively as individuals.

I recently consulted with a family about their daughter in Grade 7. Throughout the time I spent with them it was very clear that their daughter had given up on any notion of becoming a more successful student. Several times their daughter told me that there was no point to getting any help and that grades, good or bad, did nothing to motivate her. Our conversation also revealed that, where the child had once been fairly active in extracurricular activities, she now avoided things like sports. The parents simply shrugged their shoulders in response to the situation, stating that there was nothing they knew of that they could do. According to the parents, their daughter's teacher shared a simple observation: She had fallen between the cracks. The problem was that no one was facing this challenge in an attempt to get her *out* of the cracks.

This consultation, like others I have experienced, revealed many things. One of the most obvious was that the student didn't have the mental or emotional strength to try or even care about her grades. Fortitude is not something that is easily taught; it must often be built on. In the case of this particular student, if her family had taught and helped her with academic challenges in earlier grades, she could have begun building upon those experiences in order to overcome the obstacles she would encounter in middle school. Many times parents will ask me how a child can be expected to be motivated or successful if all she has experienced is academic hardship. I certainly agree that years of struggling and failure present huge challenges. We can only deal with discouragement for so long. But in many of these cases, I discover that parents either ignored their children's struggles in earlier grades, made excuses for them or, just as concerning, simply did much of the difficult work for them.

Wisdom

The word *wisdom* conjures images of ancient sages or great leaders. But even children can show wisdom. Obviously, when we're talking about children, wisdom is relative. We wouldn't claim that a 10-year-old child has the wisdom of someone much older (at least in most cases). Wisdom, for the purpose of this discussion, involves good judgment, putting good intentions into action, setting priorities and understanding what's important in life. When we view wisdom in our children in light of these parameters, it becomes clear why this is an attribute that's important for our kids to learn.

Some of the most successful students are those who have learned how to use good and sound judgment. Wise students tend to have a greater balance in their life between school and other activities. These students have made the realization that success in school can be achieved with the right attitude, effort and level of organization. They have experienced, first-hand, the satisfaction gained through conscious decisions to make the right choices when it comes to academics. Wise students also tend to have very fulfilling lives outside of school. When a student doesn't use good judgment, she can eventually fall into a pattern of laziness, poor self-esteem, strained relationships with family members and, of course, poor grades.

Wisdom is often gained through experience. That's why

when we attempt to teach our children how to be responsible by giving them meaningful tasks to complete it's not surprising that the experience also adds to a child's wisdom. On numerous occasions, I've seen the students I work with grow in wisdom simply by being given the opportunity to experience the positive outcome of hard work. Many students struggle to earn better grades in school simply because they're not organized and spend little, if any, time preparing for tests or completing projects. Most of these kids also know, deep down, that their procrastination and lack of organization are the likely culprits for their academic struggles. Yet they do nothing about it. In these cases, a student must not only be shown how to get organized but also be given the task of putting what they have been taught into action. While there may not be an immediate turnaround, change will come. This is where perseverance plays a role. The experience will not only teach the student how to get organized but that doing so actually results in better grades. It will also demonstrate to a student that not all things worth the effort result in quick fixes. These types of experiences produce wisdom in children.

Integrity

When trying to explain what integrity is, people will often state that it's what people do when they know no one else is listening or looking. In my teaching days, I would sometimes leave the classroom just to see what my students would do if I was gone for a few minutes. I would stay within earshot and listen in on the activity. Sometimes this would give me clues about individual kids or my class as a whole. I wanted to know what they would do when they believed I wasn't watching or listening. When it comes to our own children and their academics, we earnestly want them to work at being great students without our constant monitoring. When a child has integrity, a parent can have faith in her ability to work in school and at home to the best of her ability without being micromanaged.

Integrity is about being honest not only with others but also with oneself. When we say that someone has integrity, we typically see him or her as a person who is truthful, committed and true to his or her beliefs. However, a person of integrity also has the desire and self-discipline to examine herself and recognize strengths and shortcomings. This all sounds impressive but, admittedly, it is perhaps a little too much for us to expect from a child. Given this, I would suggest that it's an entirely reasonable goal for us to teach our kids to become conscientious. While it may not have the depth or complexity of self-reflection, it does involve elements of self-discipline and truthfulness.

When it comes to our children and their success in school, integrity is a key component in creating diligent students. Our hope is that, one day, our children will be able to examine their weaknesses and work toward improving them. Our desire is that our kids will come to the point where they will not make excuses for shortcomings or poor work but will be honest with themselves regarding their efforts and abilities. In the meantime, we can offer guidance on what it means to work hard, regardless of circumstances, and be honest about the effort. For example, a student who doesn't complete homework assignments and rarely prepares for tests must accept the conclusion that it's her own fault that she isn't enjoying greater success and make the changes necessary to improve.

Integrity allows a student to experience greater fulfillment in school. It doesn't allow an individual to hide from her problems but challenges her to meet them directly. It doesn't guarantee quick results but helps a student to push forward. In addition to inspiring students to reach greater heights in academics, integrity teaches children a greater sense of grace and understanding.

Within the confines of the student community, all students function at a higher level when they feel safe, accepted and encouraged. Two of the greatest obstacles toward creating and maintaining an environment where students can experience this are bullying and peer pressure. Parents expect schools to deal with these issues, but many won't take the steps necessary to ensure their child is not part of the problem. Children who have integrity will not judge other kids because those children have seen in themselves their own shortcomings. Nor will a child with integrity wrongly pressure other kids.

How Do We Teach Our Children the Intangibles?

I'm firm in my opinion that character development isn't the role of our schools. Many would disagree with me. I understand that our education system's desire to engage children in social justice and character development programs is well intentioned, but it falls short of accomplishing its goals. Developing positive character in your child begins at home.

By their very nature, qualities like wisdom, integrity and perseverance are difficult to formally teach. It's ironic that they're considered so valuable not only in academic life but life in general, yet there's no go-to program, teaching method or guidebook. Sometimes, even with our best efforts as parents, it may seem as though the positive character development we desire in our child is out of reach.

Like much of what I've discussed in this book, I believe that we should be led by common sense. Character development doesn't happen overnight, and so our approach must also be unfailingly consistent. While I don't have any tried and true methods, there are ways that we, as parents, can guide our kids in developing the intangibles that I've described.

- *Set the Example*: This isn't a new concept, but there's a reason for that. If you want a child who's honest and kind, who has integrity and a host of other positive traits, *you* need to set the example. Don't kid yourself: Your son or daughter is watching. Of course, you'll be less than perfect in your example from time to time, but as I mentioned, consistency is the key.

- *Share Your Values*: While your example serves as a template for your child to follow, don't assume that she knows what you value. In our pluralistic society, we sometimes become too careful about sharing our beliefs and values, even with our own children. Take many opportunities to share your values with your kids, especially when you come across teachable moments.

- *Show Respect for Others*: If you want your child to show kindness, tolerance and a general respect for other people, make sure you're leading the way. It can be difficult sometimes when we feel that we haven't been dealt with fairly by other people—including our own spouse or other family members—but it's precisely at these moments that our children are paying particular attention. Teach your child respect by showing respect for others.

- *Take Advantage of "Teachable Moments"*: Sometimes it's tough to find the right times to talk with your child about things like your beliefs and values, and we have to manufacture those moments. Every so often, though, the perfect teachable moment presents itself. Sometimes it's when your child asks you a certain kind of question, or you're both watching something on television, or even when you've had to discipline your child. You'll know when you're in a teachable moment, so don't shy away; take advantage of it.

- *Spend Time Together as a Family*: This is as simple as it sounds. Do it regularly and don't make the mistake of believing that the quality of the time you spend with your child is just as important, if not more so, than the quantity of time. These times together are the perfect opportunity to talk about your beliefs and values and to be an example.

- *Set Expectations and Accountability*: While our greatest desire as parents is for our kids to be happy and secure, we should never make the mistake of not setting boundaries because we're worried about how it might make our children feel. Set expectations in your home, establish boundaries (rules) and keep your son or daughter accountable. Yes, that might mean that, from time to time, you'll have to discipline your child. In fact, count on it. If your expectations aren't reflections of your values, your efforts to develop your child's character will be in vain.

- *Be the Head of the Home*: Along with setting expectations, you must be the leader in your house.

I'm talking about both Mom and Dad sharing this responsibility. Your child should never set the standard—you should. You may even have to say no once in while. Again, if you fail to lead and crumble or constantly compromise because you're afraid of disappointing your child, you'll just be spinning your wheels. Kids must be accountable to their parents.

- *Be Involved*: Get to know everything you can about your child. This includes who her friends are, the things she likes to do, the programs she likes to watch on television—everything. Too many parents deal with unpleasant surprises simply because they wished to respect their child's privacy. You can be respectful of privacy and still be informed. The easiest way to do this, of course, is by spending time with her.

Before I wrote this chapter, I had to think about whether or not it would really add to our discussion on helping your child become a better student. So often we make a clear distinction between the character of our children and their success in school. I finally decided that it wasn't only worthwhile to write about it, but it was absolutely necessary. I believe Thomas Lickona sums up my feelings on the matter best:

> All of us who are parents naturally want our children to be successful. But we know in our bones that success without *character*—qualities such as honesty, a sense of responsibility, kindness, and determination in the face of difficulty—doesn't count for much.[50]

Our child's character affects many areas of her life, and education happens to be a big one. Does it automatically mean that, if your child has integrity or perseverance or is responsible, she'll be a stellar student? No, it doesn't. But I've often noticed two truths about the relationship between a positive character and academics. First, many kids who possess the intangibles happen to be good students. Second, and more important, those kids who struggle in school must be equipped with character traits that allow them to work hard and carry on to overcome their academic challenges.

PART 3

Educating Your Child at Home

I HAVE TALKED AT SOME length about the challenges our children face in the classroom, the challenges that our education system grapples with and how we, as parents, can stand in the gap to ensure that our children are successfully educated. Any worthwhile discussion on parental involvement wouldn't be complete without a closer look at the ultimate form of parental involvement: homeschooling.

Homeschooling is an all-encompassing approach to helping your child. In fact, it requires the full effort and attention of the parents, since they're essentially taking on the responsibility of teaching their child, not just providing a little extra help. I've included this section because I've had many parents ask me about it. As you'll see, there is a tendency for those who don't know much about homeschooling to have misconceptions about what it involves and exactly what kinds of students are homeschooled.

When I use the term *homeschooling*, I use it in its broadest sense. Perhaps a more accurate description of what is actually taking place is *home-based education*. There are a number of stereotypes attached to the idea of homeschooling that I hope to dispel. In reality, there are far more options when it comes to home-based education than many people realize. The sheer number of choices in terms of resources, online classes, labs and consulting is quite surprising. Homeschooling, quite simply, offers parents a real, and sometimes superior, option when it comes to educating their children.

CHAPTER 11

The Growing Appeal of Homeschooling

THE POPULARITY OF HOMESCHOOLING HAS grown exponentially in recent years. In fact, according to the National Home Education Research Institute, over 2 million children from kindergarten to Grade 12 were being homeschooled in the United States in 2010. What's more, NHERI estimates that, in the United States, the number of homeschooled children is increasing by almost 8 percent every year.[51] While recent Canadian statistics are a little harder to come by, it's estimated that there were over 80,000 students being homeschooled in 2000. When you compare that to the number of Canadian children homeschooled in 1979, a mere 17,523, it's easy to see just how much homeschooling has grown in a relatively short period of time.[52] It's also clear that, with regard to population size, Canada is quickly catching up to the United States in terms of homeschooled students per capita.

Homeschooling, or home-based education, has grown to such a large extent that there is an entire industry dedicated to producing resources, textbooks, software and a host of other goods and services to meet the needs of the homeschooled child and her parents. Current homeschooling in no way resembles that stereotypical picture of staunchly religious families living somewhat isolated from the world, nor is it merely a means for educating those with severe learning disabilities, social ineptitudes or extreme giftedness.

There are a host of advantages and disadvantages associated with homeschooling your child. In fact, devoting just one chapter to the homeschooling option really doesn't do it justice. However, it deserves some attention for the simple fact that I am frequently asked about homeschooling, and given that the responsibility of educating a homeschooled student rests squarely on the shoulders of the parents, it is entirely relevant to our discussion on parental involvement. If you are a parent who is seriously considering homeschooling for your child, this chapter will serve as an introduction to the most important considerations. If you know that homeschooling is definitely not a fit for you and your child, you'll find these pages an interesting overview on the subject from which, hopefully, you can gain a much greater appreciation for the state of homeschooling in North America.

Why Homeschool?

In years past, it was widely believed that most families who homeschooled did so because of their religious beliefs. While there are still a large percentage of families who educate their children at home for this very reason, you may be surprised to learn that this isn't the only reason parents homeschool. In fact, it isn't even the most prevalent reason. According to NHERI, while 30 percent of families in the United States homeschool for religious reasons, over 31 percent do so because of their dissatisfaction with the public - and private - school environment.[53]

Even though homeschooling is a viable alternative to the school classroom, it isn't something parents should jump into without due consideration. While families may have a number of reasons to think about educating their son or daughter at home, there are three in particular that should be seriously considered.

Reason #1: Academics

Homeschooling can offer real academic advantages over the regular classroom. Things like one-to-one interaction, choice of resources, teaching approaches, fewer distractions and greater academic challenges are all aspects of homeschooling that, if organized effectively, can provide your child with the kind of learning that is superior to the school classroom. When the only other choice is an education system that focuses on self-esteem over performance and puts little emphasis on teaching foundational skills, homeschooling may serve as the ultimate solution for some families.

As we've observed in earlier chapters, there is a lot of time within the elementary-school day dedicated to a host of non-academic activities. While these activities may have some value, the bottom line is that they take away from time that could be spent on learning. Homeschooling is focused learning time.

Reason #2: Athletics

There are many students who are actively involved in sports or other activities at a high or elite level. The balance between school attendance, academic achievement and training can often prove too difficult to achieve. Since homeschooling is typically free of the various non-academic activities that are associated with the regular classroom, it allows students to focus on their studies while, at the same time, train and compete adequately in their chosen sport.

It's important to emphasize that simply because your child is a good athlete or has a particular interest in a sport doesn't necessarily justify pulling her from the regular classroom in favour of homeschooling. This is especially true when academics suffer in favour of training. The results can be disastrous, since in most cases, the student never achieves the level of play and recognition that the family hoped for and her schooling is severely compromised.

Reason # 3: Special Needs

While schools typically have the personnel to work with students with special needs, the unfortunate fact is that many students with diagnosed learning disabilities or other disabilities simply won't receive adequate help from the school. For parents who are well-informed regarding their children's challenges and have the patience and confidence to work with a child with special needs, homeschooling may offer the kind of environment that is well suited to meet those needs.

I emphasize the need to be well-informed since the resources and teaching approaches required may involve a degree of training and experience. However, given that homeschooling is primarily a one-to-one approach and the parents can give their undivided attention to their child's academic needs, it can provide the pace and expectations that are best suited for their son or daughter. Individual Education Plans (IEPs), while certainly a necessary and useful tool for children with special needs in the classroom, don't contain intimate knowledge of a child's specific needs. In many cases, having a teaching assistant along with a well-planned IEP is entirely sufficient for students with special needs. However, there are circumstances where a child simply requires more attention and more time from the classroom teacher, special-education teacher or teaching assistant but, due to demand or a lack of funding, it simply can't be provided.

What Are the Advantages?

Whatever a family's reason for choosing it, homeschooling can offer a number of advantages. Parents often feel that it's only within the regular classroom, among friends and peers, where a child can truly be taught. While I often counsel families to "count the cost" of homeschooling, the reality is that homeschooling, when done right, can prove to be a great choice for some kids.

One-to-One Attention

There are clear advantages to working with your child one-to-one in a learning environment. In this sense, the regular classroom simply can't compete. Time and again we hear about or have personal experience with students who fall between the cracks. This expression points to the huge challenges in ensuring that every child in a classroom of 20 to 30 students grasps the material. It's impossible to keep tabs on every child's understanding of various lessons, procedures and concepts, for the simple reason that you can't closely observe each student's attentiveness, understanding and actual work.

It's common to hear how "the lights came on" whenever kids work one-to-one with a tutor. Material that seemed to be so far out of reach when taught in the classroom suddenly made sense. The reason, quite simply, is that the tutor has the advantage of being able to discern a student's reaction—positive or negative—to the material being taught. If she seems confused, the tutor doesn't move on but identifies why the student is confused and focuses on ensuring she fully understands before moving forward. Since homeschooling moms and dads work one-to-one with their children, the same advantages can be seen.

Time

For some kids, the pace of a regular classroom environment is just too fast. As they're wrestling to grasp one lesson, the teacher moves on to the next lesson or subject. These kids end up falling further and further behind and, in a system where practice and repetition for mastery is frowned upon, never have the opportunity to catch up. While it's certainly important to have the school year mapped out, homeschooling allows parents to slow down the pace of learning in order to ensure their child not only understands new lessons but masters foundational skills in the process. There are children who tend to catch on relatively quickly and need to be more challenged. In these cases, parents have the luxury of presenting material that is more challenging (but reachable) than what is usually offered for their child's grade level and age.

Homeschooling also allows families a great deal more flexibility when it comes to family outings and vacations. In many cases, a family can save on travel costs by organizing vacations around nonpeak times and, as an added bonus, avoid many of the negatives of peak holiday travel, such as crowds, traffic and availability. Sometimes, provided that lessons have been taught and work completed, the school day can start in the morning and end by lunch. This allows for plenty of opportunities to go on field trips and afternoon family outings or simply gives a child the opportunity to play.

Values

For many families, homeschooling allows parents to teach their child in an environment where values and beliefs can be properly passed on. While it's true that, historically, homeschoolers tended to choose homeschooling for religious reasons, homeschooling is not reserved for those who have religious convictions. Even parents who are not religious are concerned about their child's values and how she treats those around her. While our schools place a strong emphasis on ridding the schoolyard of bullies; increasing students' awareness and appreciation of other cultures, creeds and beliefs; and organizing classes and discussions on issues of social justice, the school environment simply can't teach a child values, morals and ethics the way parents can. Religion-based or not, homeschooling offers the ideal environment for parents to teach and exemplify the values and beliefs that are important to them.

Greater Focus on Approaches that Work

Throughout this book, I've discussed the problem with current teaching philosophies and approaches within the average elementary classroom. For some families, simply helping their children learn and master essential skills at home after school isn't enough. They may feel that, as long as their child continues to be taught in an environment that doesn't place a premium on the mastery of procedural skills, she will never realize her true academic potential. If parents wish to focus on teaching methods and resources that are truly effective, they have the luxury of adopting those methods through homeschooling.

Socialization

Many children who are homeschooled are better socialized than those who attend regular schools. It's ironic that this is the case, since time and again, the number one concern or objection that parents have to homeschooling is the notion that children somehow won't develop proper social skills. The assumption is that a child who is not constantly surrounded by her peers will somehow lack the experiences necessary to interact normally with other people. This is based mainly on ignorance, since many individuals know so little about modern homeschooling and have never stopped to consider what proper social skills consist of and how they are effectively developed in a child.

Children who attend public or private schools associate mainly with other kids their age. It's this environment, surrounded by their inexperienced and immature peers, that we mistakenly assume is the best and only place for kids to develop social skills. We typically associate things like conflict resolution, appropriate behaviour, sensitivity and overall tolerance with proper social skills. These skills should be taught and exemplified by adults who, presumably, have already acquired them, along with the knowledge and maturity to convey them. While being around classmates may give kids the opportunity to put into practice the social skills that they're learning and being encouraged to use, it's quite another thing to somehow believe that it's through peer interaction that kids actually learn them. Homeschooling offers three distinct advantages when it comes to learning proper social skills:

1. The skills are taught and modelled through one-to-one interactions with an adult.

2. Homeschooled children have many more opportunities to develop and practice their social

skills in many different surroundings around many different types of people, including other kids.

3. Their behaviour and response to different interactions with people and various social situations can be closely monitored and quickly corrected by parents. This kind of direct and immediate feedback simply doesn't happen in the average school. Typically teachers and administration must react to unacceptable behaviour and can rarely, if ever, provide consistent and ongoing guidance in this area.

What's the Downside?

At this point, for some of you, homeschooling may sound like the best way to go. Of course, there are always two sides to every choice, and this is especially true when it comes to homeschooling. If you're thinking about educating your child at home, it's important to weigh the good and the not-so-good realities of being a homeschooling parent.

Stress

Homeschooling, particularly for those who are just starting out, can be the source of a lot of stress. The first and perhaps biggest source of stress comes from the interactions between child and parent. In fact, I haven't yet met with a homeschooling mom or dad who hasn't experienced, at least from time to time, a good deal of frustration and impatience with his or her child. When it comes to homeschooling, parents have much more than a casual interest in their child's academics, since they are also emotionally invested. It can be difficult to separate "school" talk once the school day is done from the rest of everyday life, and this, depending on the circumstances, can add to the tension.

Stress naturally arises when a child struggles with a subject or a particular lesson or concept. Parents who bear the bulk of the responsibility for teaching their child may feel as though their efforts are falling short. Moms and dads may feel guilty and inadequate if their children get stuck in an academic rut. Without the right support, homeschooling can sometimes feel like a very lonely undertaking for parents. Over time, however, with established routines, greater experience and knowledge, this feeling tends to diminish.

Peer Interactions

While I've addressed the myth that homeschooled kids tend to lack social skills, it's true that homeschooling does make peer interactions challenging at times. Friendships are an important part of any person's life, particularly for children. In school as part of a regular classroom, kids have ample opportunities to interact with their friends and form social groups. Homeschooled kids simply don't have the same daily interactions with friends.

Fortunately, there are homeschooling associations and informal groups that make a point of creating opportunities for kids to interact with each other through organized outings, gym days and so on. Sports teams and various youth clubs also offer kids the chance to be around others their age.

School Sports

For those kids who are athletically inclined and enjoy playing team sports, regular schools offer plenty of opportunities to participate in a number of sports. For kids who are homeschooled, these opportunities are difficult to come by. I say difficult and not impossible because, depending on the province or state where you live, the laws governing participation in school sports for homeschooled kids may differ. Individual schools may also have specific policies regarding their sports teams and the involvement of homeschooled students.

In my home province, for example, a child who is educated at home can either be "enrolled" or "registered." The basic difference is that, as an enrolled student who is educated at home, you would be formally enrolled in a school that offers a distributed learning program where a certified teacher closely monitors coursework, grading and learning outcomes. With registration, a parent is not required to follow the provincially mandated curriculum and a certified teacher does not monitor the student. However, the student must be registered with a local public school or a private school. Registered students may play on the school's sports teams, but enrolled students may not. My point is not to detail the list of differences between being an enrolled or a registered student, but to simply give an example of how, in British Columbia at least, the laws govern a child's participation in school sports.

Time

A lot of individuals assume that it takes less time in the day to teach a homeschooled child. In theory it can, but often, in practice, it doesn't work out that way. Parents' one-to-one interaction with their son or daughter allows for a greater degree of depth in the teaching. In other words, if your child gets stuck with a particular procedure or can't seem to grasp a new concept, you would typically go back over the material until you were satisfied that your child understood it. In a regular classroom, this simply doesn't take place, given the limited amount of time and the number of students in the classroom.

Homeschooling involves a good deal of preparation by the parents. It should not be approached haphazardly or with a "fly by the seat of your pants" attitude. That means that even when the school day is done for your child, your preparation for the next day or week is only beginning. Preparing for a new school year usually means that you begin your planning in the spring, not late summer or fall. The good news is that the more organized and prepared you are, the greater the likelihood that your efforts to teach will go smoothly.

Cost

There are costs associated with homeschooling your child. Textbooks, supplementary resources, online courses, stationery and a host of other essential and not-so-essential goods and services can start to add up. Of course, costs are determined by what you're willing, or not willing, to invest in. There is an entire industry dedicated to homeschoolers that many people are completely unaware of. The various resources and services that are available can be very useful for parents, especially when you begin to realize the breadth and depth of the resources available and how specific they are to homeschoolers. Once families begin to explore all that there is to offer, costs can really climb if parents aren't disciplined in their spending.

Depending on your province or state, there may be funds available from the government to help offset these costs. In British Columbia, for example, an enrolled elementary student who is educated at home can receive $1,000 in funding for resources. If you're considering homeschooling your child, do your homework and find out exactly what type of funding, if any, you are entitled to. It can make a real difference.

Support for Parents

One of the most frequently asked question by parents who are considering homeschooling is "Where do I start?" This question is what I like to call an "umbrella question" because it isn't easily answered in one response and typically leads to a host of other, related questions, like "What should I teach?" "What resources should I use?" "How do I plan a typical school day?" and "How do I ensure that the curriculum is completed in a given amount of time?" The answers to these questions are only the tip of the iceberg, because as parents dig deeper and deeper they begin to wonder about things like enrolment vs. registration, traditional curriculum, classical curriculum, school-based curriculum and online courses. But it doesn't end there, because in the process of trying to figure out the answers to those questions, parents will inevitably discover the seemingly endless amount of resources and approaches to every core subject. Throw in a lot of well-meaning but sometimes conflicting and confusing advice from other parents, and you can see why homeschooling can feel a bit overwhelming even before you ever actually sit down to teach your child.

Fortunately, there is support.

Online Schools

An online school can offer parents the freedom to choose their child's curriculum and resources while, at the same time, ensuring that their son or daughter eventually earns an official high-school diploma. The great thing about this option is that parents have access to professional support through the school's teachers, consultants and support staff. Many of these schools also offer online courses—a huge help for parents who might be homeschooling more than one child or feel that their child might benefit from the expertise of a teacher.

Depending on where you're from, it can be hard to discern whether an online school is the right fit. In Canada, if you plan on homeschooling your child until graduation, the path is completely manageable, but it may involve more planning and manoeuvring. If, as Canadians, a family chooses to register their child in an online academy based in the United States, they may want to first do their homework with regard to entrance requirements into Canadian universities. While their son or daughter will receive official transcripts and a diploma from an online school based in the United States, he or she may be expected to take the SAT or ACT as part of their application to a Canada-based university. The reason typically has to do with the fact that each Canadian province requires that students cover certain subjects and complete various prerequisites for graduation—such as courses on career planning and provincial exams—in order to earn a high-school diploma. Typically, when following the provincially based learning outcomes, taking the SAT or ACT is not required. Canadian families can also enrol their children in online or distance-education schools based in Canada, but in order to ensure that they receive official transcripts and the provincial graduation diploma, they will have to fulfill the learning outcomes prescribed by the Ministry of Education. For families living in the United States, registering with an online school is much more straightforward, since all students graduating from any U.S. high school must take the SAT or ACT for acceptance into a university or college.

While my goal is to give parents an overview of what online schools have to offer, it's impossible for me to cover every aspect and consideration in a few paragraphs. Taking the time to contact a few online schools is a prudent measure. Getting in touch with the admission's councillor at one or several universities to find out what their admission requirements are for students educated at home can also be very helpful. As you read on, you'll discover that there are organizations and individuals who specialize in helping families make decisions regarding home-based education and giving assistance as parents map out their child's education, including options for postsecondary schooling.

Consulting Experts

Making the decision to homeschool your child isn't an easy one. While families may feel that educating their child at home would be the best choice, whether their son or daughter is just starting kindergarten or is already attending a public or private school, simply getting started is not an easy undertaking. There are a host of decisions to be made. For many moms and dads, the list of considerations doesn't become fully apparent until they are well into homeschooling. As mentioned earlier, in Canada a child can either be an enrolled student who's educated at home or a registered homeschooler. Many parents don't know the difference or why it matters. Even those who eventually come to understand what these designations mean still may not grasp the implications. That's when a homeschool consultant can be a big help.

A homeschool consultant, as the title suggests, is an individual who can give families advice on whether or not homeschooling is the best choice for their child and how best to educate their child at home. These individuals are familiar with the ins and outs of home-based education, have a grasp of provincial or state learning outcomes, are familiar with the choices available to parents with regard to resources and can point the way when making decisions about various online options. The real benefit of a homeschool consultant is that he or she gives guidance based on a family's expressed needs, expectations and goals.

Homeschool consultants may work independently, be part of a company or organization that specializes in academic help or work as an employee of an online or distance-education school. When considering a self-employed private consultant, make sure to look into his or her qualifications. It's always a good sign if that person has homeschooled her own children. However, while having experience in educating a child at home is certainly a benefit, a consultant's expertise should also be based on professional qualifications, such as a degree in the field of education. If that person has experience teaching in a regular classroom and therefore has first-hand knowledge of challenges within the classroom and provincial or state-mandated learning outcomes, all the better.

Consultants who work for online schools are a great resource, but be wary of the fact that, as employees of these organizations, they may have a narrow perspective on home-based education. In other words, they may have an obvious bias toward the approach and philosophy espoused by the online school they work for. In many cases, parents can't get open access to a consultant unless they have registered with the school first.

Organizations that specialize in academic help and can provide homeschool consulting are another excellent option for parents. On the downside, finding such organizations may not be an easy task, since there are very few that offer much beyond simple tutoring. However, those that do exist can offer two great benefits: expertise and unbiased advice. While its certainly important to ask about the qualifications of these consultants, in many cases they're hired because they have both the experience and the qualifications. In addition, unlike self-employed consultants, they have access to resources and support staff that can enhance the services they provide. Consulting companies usually have no affiliation with a particular online school and, therefore, have no personal interest in pushing parents to go in one direction or another. If you're considering using this type of consulting company, be wary of attempts to upsell you to tutoring services. You may decide that tutoring would benefit your child, but that's a conversation for another time. It's a good sign if a company is willing to provide advice on whether or not you should even homeschool without having you commit to long-term services.

When it comes to homeschooling, the information I've provided in this chapter really only scratches the surface. Homeschooling isn't for everyone, nor should parents feel as though it's a better choice than sending their child to a public or private school. It is, however, a very legitimate option and one that more and more families across North America are exploring. The longer I'm involved in the business of education consulting, the more I come across parents who have either made the decision to homeschool or are considering it and doing their homework.

When asked, I always counsel families to take stock of their reasons for considering homeschooling. There are many myths and misconceptions, both for and against homeschooling, which parents should be aware of. If, in the end, you are one of those families that has chosen to educate your child at home—whether she's in elementary school or high school—then with time, organization and a little experience, you will find that homeschooling your child can be an overall positive and rewarding experience.

Part 4

Outside Help

Even the most dedicated, organized and diligent parents can sometimes reach a point where a little extra help is needed. While you've read about how you, as the parent, can make a big difference in your child's academics, your involvement may also mean that you might have to look for some outside help. Certainly not every family needs to explore these options, but since this book is dedicated to giving guidance to parents in the education of their children, exploring various education services is not only informative but can also be practical.

Education services—in the form of tutoring, consulting and test preparation—has been one of the fastest-growing industries over the past decade. On the positive side, this explosion of education services has given parents more choices than ever before as they search for options to help their child improve in school. However, the sheer number of options can be daunting as parents try to distinguish between one service and another. Whether you are considering private tutoring or a learning centre, it's difficult to know where you will receive the biggest return on your investment.

Parents frequently ask me whether or not some form of tutoring is the right choice for their child. In some cases, all they really need is information to help them weigh their options. A lot of these anxious moms and dads can't help but feel just a little guilty that they're looking for outside help. Some may feel their child's academic struggles are their fault, while others feel that considering tutoring is, in itself, somehow an admission of failure. Then there are parents who seek out consultants or hire tutors for their children regardless of their child's success or struggles, simply because they believe it gives their child a competitive advantage. There is a time and place when it's appropriate to consider outside help for your child. While it may not be essential, it's important to keep in mind that, under the right circumstances, outside help can make a big difference.

CHAPTER 12

Why Look for Outside Help?

THERE'S NO RULE WHEN IT comes to who should or shouldn't consider services like tutoring, consulting or test preparation. However, there are three important factors to consider.

1. *Time*: For many families, time is at a premium. Both parents might work; there may be other siblings who require attention; and the struggling child may be involved in extracurricular activities like sports, music or clubs. While Mom and Dad may be willing to work with their child, they may not have the time to devote to it. While I've dealt with the question of making time in another chapter, finding a tutor for your child may be a good option.

2. *Special Needs*: For children diagnosed with a specific learning disability, the decision to explore education services in the form of tutoring may be a prudent one. There may be specific strategies and resources that certain tutors have both the training and the experience to provide. It doesn't necessarily mean that a child with special and specific needs will always need a tutor, but it may be very useful in

the short term as the parents become more familiar with their child's learning disability, appropriate intervention and practical ways to help.

3. *Goals*: Sometimes achieving a specific goal requires the help of a tutor. Parents may hire tutors to prepare their child for provincial exams, ACTs or SATs in order to give them the best possible chance of getting into a college or university of their choice. Some students are high-level athletes who may need to put in extra training for an important event. Hiring a tutor can serve as a bridge while the student takes the extra time to train.

What Kind Of Outside Help Is Available?

Often, once parents determine that their son or daughter is in need of some kind of academic intervention, they may not be quite sure where to begin. As you begin exploring what's available, it's important to know the most common types of education services.

Tutoring

Tutoring, in its various forms, is designed to help kids when they're having trouble in certain subjects. It can be thought of as a way to supplement learning, particularly when kids must master foundational skills or essential procedures but have either fallen behind in the class or these skills have been neglected in the classroom environment. There are lots of choices when it comes to tutoring, and given how popular these services are, I will dive into this realm in far greater depth a little later in this chapter.

Consulting

There are times when parents simply need some direction as they attempt to help their kids at home. These parents may be dedicated to working with their kids before exploring tutoring. However, they may not know where to start, what resources are helpful or necessary or how best to organize their time. This is when an education consultant can be of help.

The qualifications of a consultant are very important, since you want to deal with an individual who understands and has experience with many aspects of education. Clearly you want someone who is formally trained in the field of education but, of equal importance, understands the various strengths and challenges of the education system, the benefits and weaknesses of different resources and, ultimately, how best to help parents meet their goals. In addition, some consulting services provide academic testing. While I'll address assessments and academic testing a little later, be aware that, in the right situation, they may prove to be very useful. If a consultant insists that academic testing should be performed, make sure you are clear on the reasons why. In my experience, the best consultants rarely suggest academic testing as a starting point and, in fact, may even caution parents against it before there has been adequate time and observation.

Test Preparation

There are services available that are entirely dedicated to helping students prepare for tests and exams. More specifically, these services help students get ready for provincial exams, SATs,

ACTs or any other exam necessary for high-school graduation and entrance into postsecondary school. These services are very popular and widely used. I caution parents, however, that when considering university or college for their son or daughter, it's never a good idea to rely wholly on test-prep services. A student who learns to be diligent and organized and obtains effective study skills in elementary school will find test preparation a much less arduous and stressful undertaking. Test-prep services are most useful as a means to supplement a student's preparation for acceptance into university, not as the sole means by which it's accomplished.

Choices, Choices, Choices

Tutoring is the most popular education service utilized in North America. Because of that, parents can become a little overwhelmed by the choices available to them. While I can't comment on every company or organization, I can offer an overview of the types of services available and their pros and cons.

Private Tutors

One of the most attractive elements of private tutoring is that it's usually done one-to-one. This means that your child will receive the undivided attention of the tutor. Not only does this usually result in easier management of the environment, but it also ensures that a student's individual questions and obstacles are given the utmost focus. If you have the right person working with your child—someone who is observant, good with your child's age group, keenly interested in their work, flexible and a good communicator—then your child's progress may be extraordinary. Parents can sometimes be surprised by how well their child responds to a tutor, especially since the tutor doesn't have the relationship that the parents have with their son or daughter. However, this is exactly the reason a tutor can make so much progress and often experience far less resistance than a student normally displays when parents attempt to help.

Private tutoring can also be very convenient, depending on whether or not the tutor will come to your home. In this day and age, convenience is a valuable commodity, and having one less place to go—like a learning centre—is highly attractive. Mom and Dad can feel more at ease knowing that their child is being tutored while they set about doing other things around the home.

Many learning centres follow a set program that may not be suitable for some students. Given that every child brings something different to the table in terms of his or her abilities and interests, it can be a challenge to meet the individual needs of a student in a prescribed learning program. With private tutoring, the idea is for the tutor to tailor the teaching style, the material and the outcomes to the unique needs of the student. As the tutor and student develop a good rapport, a great deal can be accomplished over time, since the tutor learns more about a particular student's habits (both good and bad), strengths, weaknesses and interests. With this kind of knowledge, the tutor can focus on areas that are particularly challenging for a student. In addition, unlike many learning centres, a good private tutor may make some astute observations that shed light on a child's academic struggles. For instance, the tutor may discover that a student's lack of organizational and study skills are the main culprits behind the poor grades. As they work together, the tutor can begin to introduce and reinforce these skills that, in turn, further accelerate the child's progress.

Private tutoring is usually less expensive than sending your child to a learning centre. This may not be the case in every circumstance, but as a general rule, parents can expect to pay less per hour. Since learning centres must invest in inventory, office space and marketing, the costs are usually passed down to the consumer. Not so for the private tutor, who doesn't typically incur these types of expenses.

There are certainly some disadvantages to private tutoring. It can be very difficult to find a tutor who is not only qualified and enthusiastic but also the right fit for your child. There are many individuals who, in an effort to earn supplemental income, turn to tutoring. Armed with a college degree, they figure that working with children is a relatively simple task. Sometimes, experience may not indicate whether someone will be a great tutor for your child. I have come across many veteran classroom teachers who were terrible tutors. However, experience does reveal where a tutor's interests lie. If, for example, an individual has a great education but can't demonstrate anywhere in their volunteer or work history that they have much of an interest in working with kids, chances are that person won't be a good fit. Even when a family has found someone who is educated, enthusiastic and experienced, many times scheduling becomes an issue, and not all private tutors will tutor in the home of the family.

Private tutors may not use or be aware of current academic materials used in the classroom. It isn't unusual for tutors to use a child's own textbooks during the tutoring sessions. While this may not be a problem in most situations, it does limit how much the tutor can prepare without having a copy of the materials being utilized. Since private tutors don't have access to the funds that a learning centre would have, they may shy away from making substantial investments in expensive texts and workbooks. This can sometimes prove to be a disadvantage, particularly when the tutor is in need of specific resources in order to help the student with writing, reading or math.

Learning Centres

Learning centres abound. In almost every suburb in North America, one can peer into the office or storefront window of any number of centres to observe groups of students working with staff members. In fact, tutoring companies and learning centres are among the fastest growing businesses in North America. Why such growth? Simply put, more and more parents don't want to take any risks with their child's education. In the minds of many moms and dads, spending money on their child's education isn't a luxury but a necessity. Many larger learning centres have done a remarkable job of appealing to this sense of dissatisfaction and urgency.

Learning centres can be very appealing to parents. Not only are they relatively easy to locate (unlike a good private tutor), but they also offer "one-stop shopping." Academic testing, an academic plan, resources and a trained staff member can all be found under one roof. While a set program may not benefit every student, it does use professionally developed materials. Many also offer online tutoring to meet the demands of families concerned with the inconvenience of driving to and from the learning centre. Once families agree to a schedule, they can rest assured that, each time their child is dropped off at the centre, there will be a staff member ready to facilitate the learning time.

Learning centres offer something else that attracts prospective clients: the promise of success in a given amount of time. Not only do many parents wish to see their child receive some kind of academic help, they want their son or daughter's academic woes to be cured within a certain time frame. Unlike most private tutors, learning centres have developed formulas to meet this demand. It gives parents a much greater sense of relief to know that there is an eventual end, and, hopefully, it will result in better grades for their child. Unfortunately, this can often result in disappointment, since the realities of the classroom, the resources utilized by the schools and the provincial or state-mandated learning outcomes can create a distinct gap between the outcomes experienced at the learning centre and the success a child actually has in the classroom. In other words, while the learning centre may be insisting that, according to its criteria, a child is learning and improving, it doesn't necessarily mean that the "improvement" will carry over into the classroom.

Since there are a number of learning centres to choose from, parents are often uncertain which one will best meet the academic needs of their son or daughter. Most appear to advertise the same claims about improved grades and greater confidence, and almost as many have programs that, though they appear different on the surface, essentially offer similar approaches. So what differentiates one centre from the next? Basically, the single biggest reason why some learning centres succeed over others is marketing. Television commercials, radio ads, newspaper ads and Internet advertising are all used to get the brand and message to potential clients. The marketing campaigns are carefully timed, since there are certain times of the year when parents might have the most interest in their services (such as report-card time).

Does this mean that parents should be suspicious of learning centres and their marketing efforts? No, but they should do their homework. This can start with a conversation with a classroom teacher or with friends who have had tutoring for their child. Find out the credentials of the manager or owner of the centre. Does he or she have a background in education, such as teaching, or has the individual's experience been strictly in business and marketing? This doesn't necessary mean that a learning centre isn't a good fit, but it does give an indication as to where the manager/owner's interests really lie. What are the qualifications of the teaching/tutoring staff? Be wary of businesses that claim that all of their staff are "certified," since this may only mean that their tutors have been trained in their system and not necessarily university trained and certified classroom teachers. Are there costs that the learning centre is not upfront about, such as mandatory academic assessments? These assessments can be a useful tool but are often developed by the centre with little connection to the provincial or state curriculum. If you feel that a centre isn't being very informative regarding the need and usefulness of these assessments, that's a sign to look elsewhere.

Another possible downside to learning centres is the lack of one-to-one attention. Many will make claims about "individualized attention," but phrases like this can be deceiving. "Individualized attention" doesn't mean one-to-one attention. In reality, your child could be working with a group of three or four other students and, in many cases, children from different grades and in need of help in different subject areas. Of course, the ratio of three or four students per tutor is far better than the ratio found in your average classroom. This may be more a matter of personal preference for parents, but it's important to be aware of the exact kind of attention your child will receive.

For those families where cost is a primary consideration, a learning centre may prove to be too expensive. Most of these businesses charge more per hour than private tutors. However, the added expense may be well justified, especially when one considers the possible difficulty of finding a well-matched and qualified tutor. Many parents also feel much more at ease dealing with a well-established and professional business that screens its staff and where formal contracts serve to protect the business, its staff and the families. Many private tutors don't give much consideration to various details, such as legal chaperones, late and cancellation policies and methods of payment. In fact, many qualified private tutors give up their tutoring in order to work for a learning centre or tutoring company, even at a much smaller rate of pay, just to escape from the headaches of dealing with the business end of things. Some learning centres offer payment plans for those who can't pay high monthly fees or an out-of-reach lump-sum fee. For some, this can prove to be very helpful, but I advise families to understand exactly what they're committing to.

Tutoring Companies

Tutoring companies, like private tutors, can offer one-to-one tutoring. Parents can, more or less, deal with a professional company that has policies and procedures in place to protect the parents as consumers and ensure a certain standard of quality control when it comes to the qualifications of the tutors, something they can't do with private tutors. I say "more or less" because professionalism and standards vary greatly from one company to the next.

The real benefit of a tutoring company is the one-to-one attention your child receives. Companies also offer greater convenience over a typical learning centre, since the tutor a company provides will usually come to your home. Tutoring companies often utilize the resources your child brings home from school. What this means is that the help a child receives is usually directly connected to the expectations of the classroom teacher. A tutoring company completes background checks on all its tutors, another advantage over private tutoring. In addition, if a family should need to change tutors for any reason, the tutoring company can usually accomplish this in a relatively short time period and with little headache for the family. Finally, many (but not all) tutoring companies are a little less expensive than the average learning centre.

Tutoring companies tend to offer very similar services, such as in-home tutoring, and have business models and methods that are almost identical. This isn't necessarily a bad thing, but it tends to make distinguishing one company from another a bit challenging. With little overhead and a simple business plan that has proven to be successful—as evidenced by the existence of so many other cookie-cutter tutoring companies—these operations tend to attract entrepreneurs who have little if any background in education. I have come across a number of tutoring companies, both large and small, whose founders have a background in business and marketing. Every company needs expertise in these fields, but in some cases the reason for establishing the company was, first and foremost, about applying a formula for turning a profit. Not surprisingly, the companies with the most aggressive marketing attract the greatest attention.

It is often the norm for tutoring companies to try to be all things to all people. This means they offer tutoring for all grade levels in all subject areas. On the positive side, this makes things relatively easy for parents since, like learning centres, it feels like one-stop shopping. However, such a broad focus sometimes means that the quality of service, particularly in the level of expertise, is watered-down. While perhaps not as convenient, tutoring companies that are more narrow in the services they offer, such as grade levels and subject areas, tend to have a sharpened and concentrated focus. They have the benefit of being able to offer guidance and advice that is specific and relevant to a family's particular circumstances and needs.

I make a point of highlighting theses aspects of tutoring companies not to disparage them, but to give you a starting point with which you can decide on which tutoring company, if any, is the best fit for your child. The right tutoring company can be invaluable to you and your child's education. Besides looking for a company where the owners have a background in education, I recommend searching for ones that seem to really understand what goes on in the classroom, the challenges that teachers face, and the strengths and weaknesses of the education system. This not only demonstrates a certain level of experience and expertise, it also indicates that a company—or at least those in charge—has dug deeper and given considerable thought to the challenges your son or daughter faces. In my opinion, this should be apparent after one phone call.

School-Based Programs

School-based academic help can come in the form of peer tutoring, after-school groups with teachers, reading programs facilitated by parent volunteers and any other activity that takes place within the walls of the school and is organized by the teachers and administration. Programs like these give parents a sense of confidence and peace of mind, since the impression is that anything that is sanctioned and takes place within the school must be effective.

School-based tutoring and peer-help programs can be very helpful for those students in need of some review or test preparation. For those students who are relatively strong academically but are "stuck" on a concept or lesson, these programs may be an excellent fit. Considerations like learning preference and study and organization skills are seldom factors for students who benefit from school-based tutoring; most often, all they need is a nudge in the right direction with a little time and practice in order to master a challenging concept. For parents who can't afford to pay for a private tutor or register with a learning centre, school-based programs are a logical choice.

In situations where students are tutored, either one-to-one or in groups, by their classroom teacher, even more benefits become apparent. Since a classroom teacher would normally have a good understanding of a student's particular struggles, there can be greater focus on the student's specific needs. In addition, the teacher is intimately familiar with the classroom resources (such as textbooks) and the learning outcomes for the subject area. Sometimes, when a student displays determination and diligence, the teacher may consider those factors when it comes to final grading.

Peer-tutoring programs are often of greater benefit to the tutor. It has been demonstrated that students who teach or tutor other students are, in turn, more successful in their studies. Teaching has a way of reinforcing concepts in the mind of the peer tutor. That's why, in some schools, even at-risk students will tutor other students. The role of tutor often inspires these students to take their duties seriously; since they're being relied upon to help others, they take a much more diligent approach to their own studies in order to successfully teach and review concepts with their peers. In some schools and districts, peer tutoring is used as a tool to not only help struggling students but to provide effective assistance to students at risk.

Peer tutoring, while a good way to utilize the academic strength and enthusiasm of more successful students to provide help for those who need it, can often fall short of expectations. The greatest disadvantage peer tutors have is in maturity, training and experience. The most common complaint among parents is that peer tutors seldom have the patience to work effectively with their child. The problem lies in the fact that peer tutors don't have the experience and expertise to recognize and respond according to the individual needs of the students they are working with. Most school-sanctioned peer-tutoring programs are designed with protocols that include teacher supervision and implementation. The unfortunate reality is that these programs tend to suffer from incomplete implementation and an eventual laxity in close monitoring by school staff because of a host of other demands on their time.

Unfortunately, for a great number of students, school-based tutoring programs and peer tutoring don't meet their specific academic needs. As mentioned, while these programs can prove to be a great help to already academically strong students in need of some extra help, they seldom serve to provide a long-term solution for students who struggle year after year. Of course, reading programs and other volunteer-driven initiatives within the school have value and certainly a far greater benefit than nothing at all.

While school-based programs offer the least expensive alternative—little or no cost at all—very few go through the process of evaluating, planning and tracking a student's needs and progress. It is not that these programs don't have a loose framework through which some form of evaluation and follow-up can take place, just that these good intentions tend to fall to the wayside as the demands of teaching begin to take away the focus of the school staff.

A Word on Testing and Assessments

Inevitably, whenever parents are looking for outside help, the question of academic assessments crosses their minds. It's normal to want to know where your child is at in a particular subject in comparison to her peers or by the standards and expectations of her grade level. With so much opinion on how kids should learn, what they should learn and when they should learn it, it can be very hard for parents to know exactly how their child is performing academically. Academic assessments offer insight into a child's level of understanding in a particular subject area and specific area of need.

The value of assessments depends upon the purpose and, ultimately, the need for such a test. Many learning centres require parents to pay for an assessment even before they will give recommendations for academic help. It is under these circumstances that I caution parents to be most wary. More often than not, tutoring companies and learning centres that make academic assessments a requirement and not an option are looking to add to their bottom line. Assessments, though sometimes helpful, usually tell parents what they already know and are a means of justifying expensive prepaid contracts.

My advice? Look for companies that offer academic assessments but don't require them. Also, find out what the assessment is actually designed to do. Is the test a recognized assessment, widely used with success by various professional educators, counsellors and school districts? Or is it used exclusively by or designed specifically for a certain tutoring company or learning centre? Chances are, if the assessment is an in-house type of test, it should be avoided. I believe that any assessment should be administered, if at all, only after a tutor or consultant has worked with a child over a period of time. In the majority of cases, assessments are entirely unnecessary, since teachers and parents already have a firm idea with regard to what area the child struggles in academically.

Outside help, such as tutoring or consulting services, can be a real benefit for kids who are struggling and for parents who are concerned and frustrated. While I believe that a child's academic success starts at home, there are times when a little outside help is an appropriate response to ensure that your child doesn't fall between the cracks academically. Do a quick Internet search for tutoring help where you live, and you'll likely discover a host of companies and organizations eager to provide their services. Do your homework, find out what each service has to offer and, just as importantly, be realistic about the claims some companies and individuals make.

Speak with your child's classroom teacher to get suggestions and advice. Be sure to balance your teacher's recommendations with your own goals. Often, the classroom teacher can give you some perspective on your child's academics. Sometimes, however, the teacher may play down your son or daughter's struggles. Regardless, if you decide to hire a tutor or consultant or register your child with a learning centre, it's always a good decision to keep your child's teacher in the loop. In the end, it's important to remember that you should view any outside help as an option, not a necessity.

Conclusion

Let Common Sense Be Your Guide

As I was working on this final chapter, I had the opportunity to speak with a young teacher fresh out of teacher's college. I asked her to tell me about the greatest challenge she encountered during her practicum. Interestingly, she told me it involved a particular day when she was trying to teach a math lesson on multiplying decimals. She explained that the math program the class followed was inquiry-based and, therefore, her job was to help lead the class of Grade 6 students to understand the concept. She went on to tell me that she could have easily taught the students how to actually "do" the math by teaching them directly, but she felt it was important to make sure they understood the big picture. The end result, she sighed, was that it was one of the worst teaching experiences she had in her practicum because she couldn't say with any degree of confidence that her students learned much, if anything, in math that day. On that particular day she felt, perhaps, that she wasn't cut out to teach.

The story of this young teacher wasn't necessarily new, but it was what followed that intrigued me. I asked her, point-blank, if she felt there was value in setting aside the procedural skills necessary to successfully answer a question involving the multiplication of decimals in favour of helping her students see the big picture. At first, she responded by explaining that, by focusing on conceptual understanding, the kids would understand how and why they got to their answers. I pressed further and asked if it *made sense* to expect those students to grasp a concept without having a grasp of the necessary procedures in order to answer a problem correctly. She thought about this for a moment and answered with an emphatic *no*.

My conversation with this young teacher reveals a disturbing truth about the environment our teachers are trained in. In essence, they are asked to suspend their own common sense and buy into teaching methods and philosophies that are long on good intentions but short on common sense. Michael C. Zwaagstra, Rodney A. Clifton and John Clifford Long, in their book *What's Wrong with Our Schools and How We Can Fix Them*, sum it up best:

> Why should our notion of common sense guide the effort to improve public education? The short answer is that too many current policies and practices in schools reflect the abandonment of common sense. The wisdom of practical experience and tradition too often have been trivialized or dismissed by the romantic progressives. Perhaps with the best of intentions, the progressives have allowed their enthusiasm for certain policies and practices to exceed the limitations of their evidence, and have allowed their ideology to overtake caution when it comes to the limitations of educational theory and research. In short, the superiority of their approach has not been adequately justified.[54]

As a parent, you are not powerless. Too often, we are lulled into either a false sense of security because we believe that no news is good news or a feeling that we don't have the training or expertise to make a difference. Even when we push past these discouraging suggestions, we are convinced that the time and effort involved would be enormous. While your time and effort are necessary, I hope that you've come to see that the help you can provide your child will not only be extremely effective but also far less time-consuming than you might have first expected.

While education consulting and tutoring can be useful resources, always remember that you, the parent, are the most important variable in ensuring your child is effectively and successfully educated. I hope that this book has given you the insight and guidance you need to confidently work with your child. In the end, you will instil in your son or daughter what our education system often falls short of: academic success that leads to confidence, a lifelong love for learning and a mind that can think critically. Above all, use some common sense.

Notes

[1] Malcolm Gladwell, *The Tipping Point: How Little Things Can Make a Big Difference* (Boston: Little, Brown, 2000), p. 258.

[2] Merriam-Webster Online, s.v. "common sense," accessed May 22, 2013, http://www.merriam-webster.com/dictionary/common%20sense.

[3] Jeanne S. Chall, *The Academic Achievement Challenge: What Really Works in the Classroom?* (New York: Guilford Press, 2000), p. 129.

[4] Kate Hammer, "Canadian Parents Give Report Cards a Failing Grade," *Globe and Mail*, June 28, 2012, http://www.theglobeandmail.com/news/national/parents-give-school-report-cards-a-failing-grade/article4378879/.

[5] Canadian University Survey Consortium, *2010 First-Year University Student Survey*, June 2010, p. 61, http://www.cusc-ccreu.ca/publications/2010_CUSC_firstYr_Master.pdf.

[6] Gregory K. Tippin, Kathryn D. Lafreniere and Stewart Page, "Student Perception of Academic Grading: Personality, Academic Orientation, and Effort," *Active Learning in Higher Education* 13, 1 (March 2012), pp. 51–61.

[7] Tippin, Lafreniere and Page, p. 58.

[8] Maureen Stout, *The Feel-Good Curriculum: The Dumbing Down of America's Kids in the Name of Self-Esteem* (Cambridge, MA.: Perseus Books, 2000), p. 163.

[9] Chall, p. 122.

[10] Jean M. Twenge, *Generation Me: Why Today's Young Americans Are More Confident, Assertive, Entitled—and More Miserable Than Ever Before* (New York: Free Press, 2006), p. 2.

[11] Twenge, p. 218.

[12] Twenge, p. 57.

[13] Stout, pp. 1–2.

[14] Margaret M. Clifford, "Students Need Challenge, Not Easy Success," *Educational Leadership* (September 1990), p. 22.

[15] Mark Bauerlein, *The Dumbest Generation: How the Digital Age Stupefies Young Americans and Jeopardizes Our Future (or, Don't Trust Anyone Under 30)* (New York: Jeremy P. Tarcher/Penguin, 2008), pp. 8–9.

[16] "Teacher Education Program Transforms Students into Teachers With a Social Justice Focus," *Abbotsford News*, October 18, 2010, p. A2.

[17] Rita Kramer, *Ed School Follies: The Miseducation of America's Teachers* (New York: Free Press, 1991), p. 210.

[18] Joyce Cooper-Kahn and Laurie C. Dietzel, *Late, Lost, and Unprepared: A Parents' Guide to Helping Children with Executive Functioning* (Bethesda, MD: Woodbine House, 2008), p. 17.

[19] Cooper-Kahn and Dietzel, p. 5.

[20] National Education Association, *Policy Brief: Technology in Schools: The Ongoing Challenge of Access, Adequacy and Equity* (Washington, DC: Center for Great Public Schools, 2008).

[21] BC Ministry of Education, *Kindergarten Curriculum Package* (Victoria, B.C.: BC Ministry of Education, 2010).

[22] BC Ministry of Education, *Curriculum Package for Grade 3, 4, 5, 6, and 7* (Victoria, B.C.: BC Ministry of Education, 2010).

[23] Richard E. Clark, Paul A. Kirschner and John Sweller, "Putting Students on the Path to Learning: The Case for Fully Guided Instruction," *American Educator* 36 (Spring 2012), p. 6.

[24] E. D. Hirsch, Jr., *The Schools We Need and Why We Don't Have Them* (New York: Doubleday, 1996), p. 134.

[25] Clark, Kirschner and Sweller, p. 6.

[26] John Jarolimek and Clifford Donald Foster, *Teaching and Learning in the Elementary School* (New York: Macmillan, 1976), p. 142.

[27] Clark, Kirschner and Sweller, p. 8.

[28] Harold Pashler, Mark McDaniel, Doug Rohrer and Robert Bjork, "Learning Styles: Concepts and Evidence," *Psychological Science in the Public Interest* 9, 3 (December 2008), pp. 107–108.

[29] Steven A. Stahl, "Different Strokes for Different Folks? A Critique of Learning Styles," *American Educator* (Fall 1999), p. 1.

[30] Vicki Snider, *Myths and Misconceptions About Teaching: What Really Happens in the Classroom* (Lanham, Maryland: Rowman & Littlefield Education, 2006), p. 120.

[31] Clark, Kirschner, and Sweller, p. 6–11.

[32] Snider, p. 120.

[33] Keith Devlin, "How Do We Learn Math?" *Devlin's Angle* (blog), *Mathematical Association of America*, March 2006, http://www.maa.org/devlin/devlin_03_06.html.

[34] Hung-His Wu, "Basic Skills Versus Conceptual Understanding: A Bogus Dichotomy in Mathematics Education," *American Educator* (Fall 1999), p. 1.

[35] John Mighton, *The End of Ignorance: Multiplying Our Human Potential* (Toronto: A. A. Knopf Canada, 2007), p. 62.

[36] Deb Russell, "Dispelling the Math Myths," *About.com Mathematics*, accessed September 12, 2012, http://math.about.com/cs/mathreform/a/myths.htm.

[37] Mighton, p. 64.

[38] Cynthia Reynolds, "Why Is It Your Job to Teach Your Kid Math?" *Maclean's*, March 13, 2012, http://www2.macleans.ca/2012/03/13/have-you-finished-your-homework-mom/.

[39] W. Stephen Wilson, "In Defense of Mathematical Foundations," *Educational Leadership* (March 2011), p. 72.

[40] E. D. Hirsch, Jr., *The Knowledge Deficit: Closing the Shocking Education Gap for American Children* (Boston: Houghton Mifflin, 2006), p. 8.

[41] Sebastian Wren, "Sight Word Reading," *BalancedReading.com*, accessed October 30, 2012, http://www.balancedreading.com/sightword.html.

[42] Catherine E. Snow and Connie Juel, "Teaching Children to Read: What Do We Know About How to Do It?" *The Science of Reading: A Handbook*, edited by Margaret J. Snowling and Charles Hulme (Malden, MA: Blackwell Publishing Ltd., 2005), p. 507.

[43] Linnea C. Ehri, Simone R. Nunes, Dale M. Willows, Barbara Valeska Schuster, Zohreh Yaghoub-Zadeh and Timothy Shanahan, "Phonemic Awareness Instruction Helps Children Learn to Read: Evidence from the National Reading Panel's Meta-Analysis," *Reading Research Quarterly* 36, 3 (July/August/September 2001), p. 274.

[44] Chall, p. 61.

[45] Kate Nation, "Children's Reading Comprehension Difficulties," *The Science of Reading: A Handbook*, edited by Margaret J. Snowling and Charles Hulme (Malden, MA: Blackwell Publishing Ltd., 2005), p. 254.

[46] Chall, p. 66.

[47] Hirsch, p. 8.

[48] Hirsch, p. 12.

[49] Hirsch, p. 2.

50 Thomas Lickona, *Character Matters: How to Help Our Children Develop Good Judgment, Integrity, and Other Essential Virtues* (New York: Simon & Schuster, 2004), p. 4.

51 "Homeschool Population Report," *National Home Education Research Institute*, accessed December 5, 2012, http:/www.nheri.org/research/nheri-news/homeschool-population-report-2010.html.

52 Patrick Basham, John Merrifield and Claudia R. Hepburn, "Homeschooling: From the Extreme to the Mainstream," *Studies in Education Policy*, October 2007, p. 9.

53 "The Positive Reality of Homeschooling Statistics," *Homeschool-Companion,* accessed January 20, 2013, http://www.homeschool-companion.com/homeschooling-statistics.html.

54 Michael C. Zwaagstra, Rodney A. Clifton and John Clifford Long, *What's Wrong with Our Schools and How We Can Fix Them* (Lanham, MD: Rowman & Littlefield Education, 2010), pp. 179–180.

Index

A

About.com, 94
academic problems, compounding of, 59–60
academic success
    effort and, 12, 167
    intangibles and, 5, 163
    mastery and, 42
    as means, not end goal, 19
    self-esteem and, 15, 23
    as starting at home, 215
    willpower and, 169
The Academic Achievement Challenge (Chall), 8, 120
accomplishments
    feeling good about selves and, 4
    value of, 23, 24
accountability, 152, 176
achievement gaps, 46, 79
achievement indicators, 41–42, 50–51
active classroom, 54
Active Learning in Higher Education, 15
activities, prioritization of, 141, 150
ACTs, preparation for, 204
addition, 64, 99, 103
album covers, 46, 58, 67, 74

algebra, 97
American Educator, 56
application
    neglect of, 58
    of teaching training, 30
    of tools, 133
arithmetic, 99–100
assessments. *See also* evaluations
    avoidance of objective ones, 6
    as fuzzy and subjective, 58
    impact of vague curriculum on, 44
    lack of, 50
    at learning centres, 209
    myth of learning skills assessment, 80–82
    outside help with, 214–215
    for phonics, 125
    of projects, 58
    self-assessments, 10
    as watered-down, 10–11
assumptions parents have about education
    #1: teaching/learning has advanced, 26–27
    #2: teachers as expert in all subject areas, 28–30
    #3: students as being taught essential learning skills, 31–32

#4: learning assistance as effective for all struggling students, 32–33
#5: students as engaged in learning all day, 33–34
#6: technology as widely and effectively used, 34–36
#7: elementary school as adequate preparation, 36–37
as needing to be questioned, 37
athletics, 100, 183–184, 190–191
authentic approach to teaching, 93, 94
authentic learning, 63

B

BalancedReading.com, 114
Bauerlein, Mark, 26
BC Ministry of Education, 41
behaviour, schools as teaching children about, 7
behavioural issues, in classroom, 6–7
behaviourism, 28
Bjork, Robert, 75
blackboards, 34
bodily-kinaesthetic intelligence, 72
brain-based learning, 28
brainstorming, 158, 159
breaking it down, as tool, 159–160
British Columbia, learning outcomes, 41, 47–49
bullying, 7, 163, 174

C

calculators, 8–9, 55, 61, 103, 107
calendars, 132, 134–135
"Canadian Parents Give Reports a Failing Grade," 12
Canadian University Survey Consortium (CUSC), 14–15
Chall, Jeanne S., 8, 17, 120, 121
character development, 22, 174
character traits, 163–178
child-centred learning, 54, 62. *See also* learner-centred approach; student-centred approach
Clark, Richard E., 56, 58, 69, 83
classroom
  management of, 6
  physical makeup of, 74
Clifford, Margaret M., 23
Clifton, Rodney A., 218
clocks, digital, 134
clubs/organizations, 141
collaborative learning, 54, 60
college, students' inadequate preparation for, 46–47, 99
commitment, importance of, xvii
common sense
  definition, xiv
  schools as having turned backs on, 53
competition, discouragement of, 6
computer classes/labs, 36
computer programs, for practicing math concepts, 155
computers
  as organizational tool, 132–133
  tablet computers, 34, 35, 134

conceptual understanding, 59, 63, 87, 88, 90, 91, 96, 97, 99, 107, 218
constructivism, 28, 54
consulting, 199–200, 202–203
Cooper-Kahn, Joyce, 31, 32
cover art, 46, 58, 67, 74
criticism, 18–20
cueing (reading approach), 115–116
curriculum
    controversy over, 43
    discovery as more important than mastery, 43–44
    emphasis of on interests, abilities, areas of intelligence, 44
    importance of specificity in, 51
    knowledge/information as constantly changing, 44–45
    vagueness of, 39–42, 45–52
CUSC (Canadian University Survey Consortium), 14–15

D

day planners, 132, 133, 134
decoding (in reading), 40, 112, 113, 114, 118–120, 122, 124, 125, 129
Devlin, Keith, 89–90
Dietzel, Laurie C., 31, 32
digital clocks, 134
dioramas, 44, 46, 58
direct instruction
    and discovery learning, 54, 60, 64
    as frowned upon, 43–44, 87
    impact of lack of, 60, 63, 93
    importance of, 90
    new math and, 92
    as one cornerstone for teaching math, 100
    and teacher as facilitator, 59
discovery learning
    arguments for exclusive use of, 62–68
    discovery as more important than mastery, 43–44
    as new approach, 27
    philosophy of, 54–56
    realities of, 56–61
discovery-based math, 87, 93, 98
division, 64, 97, 99, 103
Dolch, E. W., 114
drill and kill, 66–67, 101
drills and practice, 44, 60, 87, 90, 92, 100–101
The Dumbest Generation (Bauerlein), 26
dumbing down, 9

E

Ed School Follies (Kramer), 29
education, philosophies of. *See* philosophies in education
education services, 199
Educational Leadership, 23, 99
effort
    as intangible, 164, 166–168
    over performance, 12–14, 22, 96
    as subjective and impossible to quantify, 16
    as ultimately producing results, 24

electronic devices, cautions with, 134
electronic organizers, 132
encouragement, 23–24
evaluations. *See also* assessments
    inequality of in individual learning style approach, 78–79
    lack of consistency and objectivity in, 11
exams, as more and more rare, 10. *See also* quizzes; tests
expectations
    different and conflicting, 61
    importance of high ones, 24
    lowering of, 8–9
    setting of, 176
exploration, 54

F

failure, as okay, 9, 22, 23, 167, 168
false sense of security, parents as lulled into, 218–219
The Feel-Good Curriculum (Stout), 15
feelings, and constructive criticism, 19–20
filers, portable, 135
flash cards, 155
flexibility
    in homeschooling, 186
    pros and cons of, 50, 51
fortitude, as intangible, 169–171
free writing, 9, 64

G

Gardner, Howard, 72, 73
Generation Me (Twenge), 18
Gladwell, Malcolm, xiii–xiv
global (reading approach), 113
Globe and Mail, 12
grading, 10–15
grammar, 9, 46, 47, 64, 80, 159
gratification
    immediate gratification/instant gratification, 22, 178
    positive gratification, 22
group collaboration, 60
grouped desks, 54, 77

H

hands-on learning, 54, 67, 94
hard work, 4, 9, 23, 31, 37, 96, 99, 112, 149–150, 166, 167, 172
higher-order thinking skills, 27, 53, 54, 63, 64–65, 88, 89, 90, 103
Hirsch, E. D., Jr., 57, 112, 124, 129
home-based education, 179
homeschool consultants, 195–196
homeschooling
    advantages of, 185–189
    appeal of, 181–182
    definition, 179
    downside of, 189–192
    reasons why, 182–184
    support for, 193–197
homework, 33–34, 132–133, 136, 138–143, 149–152, 154–155, 160, 165, 166, 170, 173
homework boards, 32

I

IEPs (Individual Education Plans), 184
immediate gratification/instant gratification, 22, 168
important information, organizing and remembering of, 153–155
incremental learning
   of math, 96–98, 102, 104
   of reading, 125–126
Individual Education Plans (IEPs), 184
individual learning styles, 6, 71–84
inflated self-view, 20–22
information
   important, organizing and remembering of, 153–155
   sorting through, 155–160
initiative, 31
inquiry-based learning, 54
inquiry-based math, 87
instant gratification/immediate gratification, 22, 168
intangibles (character traits), 163–178
integrity, as intangible, 164, 172–174
intelligence, impact of, 31
intelligences, multiple (MI), 28, 72–74
interpersonal intelligence, 72–73
intolerance, 7
intrapersonal intelligence, 73

J

Juel, Connie, 115
JUMP Math, 106

K

Kirschner, Paul A., 56, 58, 69, 83
knowledge
   helping children acquire, 127–129
   importance of in reading, 122–124
knowledge-based education, 124
The Knowledge Deficit (Hirsch), 112
Kramer, Rita, 29

L

language arts
   PLOs in British Columbia Grades 3–7, 47–49
   teaching of with discovery approach, 56
laptops, 34, 35
Late, Lost, and Unprepared (Cooper-Kahn and Dietzel), 31
learner-centred approach, 116. *See also* child-centred learning; student-centred approach
learning
   as skill, 131–147
   window for, 33
learning assistance, 32–33
learning centres, 207–210
learning disabilities, 32–33, 153, 182, 184, 201–202
learning how to learn, 62, 63, 78
learning outcomes. *See also* PLOs (prescribed learning objectives)

BC Ministry of Education,
  3–7, 41, 47–49
 vagueness of, 39–42
learning preferences, 82
learning skills, 31–32
learning styles
 individual, 6, 71–84
 and self-esteem, 75–76
"Learning Styles: Concepts and Evidence" (Pashler, McDaniel, Rohrer, and Bjork), 75
learning-style assessment tests, 81
length of school day, 34
Lickona, Thomas, 177
linguistic intelligence, 72
literacy, 111, 113, 114, 120
logical-mathematical intelligence, 72
Long, John Clifford, 218
look and say (reading approach), 113
lyrics, 44, 58, 67, 74

M

Maclean's magazine, 98
mastery, 28, 30, 39, 43–44, 58, 66, 89, 96, 99, 101, 102, 104, 118–124, 159, 186, 187. *See also* procedural understanding/mastery
math
 cornerstones for teaching of, 100–102
 inquiry-based/discovery-based, 87, 93, 98
 new math. *See* new math
 parent's role in their child's mastery of, 102–109
 resources, 105–107
 students as struggling with basic, foundational concepts, 55, 62
 teaching of in incremental manner, 96–98, 102, 104
 teaching of in individual learning style approach, 79–80
 teaching of with discovery approach, 55, 64
 textbooks, 62–63
McDaniel, Mark, 75
memorization
 breaking it down as tool for, 159–160
 as challenging limits of students' working memory, 119
 as discouraged, 27, 44, 60, 87, 92
 of times tables, 8–9
Merriam-Webster Dictionary, xiv
Mighton, John, 92, 97
mnemonics, 159
models, 56, 58–59, 74
Mozart, Amadeus, 66
multiple intelligences (MI), 28, 72–74
multiplication, 64, 97, 99, 103
music, 100, 140, 141, 201
musical intelligence, 72
Myths and Misconceptions about Teaching (Snider), 82

N

narcissism, 20
Nation, Kate, 120
National Education Association, 35
National Home Education Research Institute (NHERI), 181, 182
new math
  bad news about, 89–91
  good news about, 88–89
  inconvenient truth of, 95–98
  overview, 87–88
  reasons for championing of, 91–95
no-fail policy, 16
non-essential activities, 34
note-taking, 31

O

objective assessment and evaluation, avoidance of, 6
one-size-fits-all approach to teaching, 73–74
one-to-one attention, from teacher, 45–46
online schools, 193–194
organization
  as learning skill, 31, 131–132
  of space, 136–138
  tools for, 132–135
outside help
  described, 199–200
  kinds of, 202–204
  reasons to look for, 201–202

P

parental interest, importance of, 127–128
parents
  assumptions parents have about education. *See* assumptions parents have about education
  as lulled into false sense of security, 218–219
  roles of, in children's education. *See* parents' roles
  willingness of as greatest qualification for participating in child's education, 85
parents' roles
  in child's mastery of math, 102–109
  in child's mastery of reading, 124–127
  in follow-up (studying process), 152–153
  in previewing (studying process), 150–151
  in reviewing (studying process), 151–152
  in teaching intangibles, 174–178
Pashler, Harold, 75
patience, importance of, xvii, 164
PDA, 134
peer feedback, 10
peer pressure, 174
peer tutoring, 212, 213–214
performance
  effort over, 12–14

and new-math approach, 88
perseverance
   importance of, 22–23
   as intangible, 164, 168–169
   lack of ability for, 22–23
philosophies in education. *See also* teaching approaches
   discovery-based approach. *See* discovery learning; discovery-based math
   individual learning styles, 6, 71–84
   knowledge-based education, 124
   multiple intelligences, 28, 72–74
   self-esteem movement, 1, 3–24
phonics, 9, 118–122, 125, 129
planners, 32, 132, 133, 134
PLOs (prescribed learning outcomes), 41–42
portable filers, 135
portfolios, 10
positive character development, 22, 174
positive gratification, 22
posters, 46, 58, 67, 68, 78
postsecondary education, students' inadequate preparation for, 46–47, 99
PowerPoint, 74
practice and drills, 44, 60, 87, 90, 92, 100–101
pre-primer (word lists), 113
prescribed learning outcomes (PLOs), 41–42

previewing (studying process), 150–151
primer (word lists), 113
prior knowledge/experience (reading approach), 116–117
prioritization of activities, 141, 150
private tutors, 204–207
proactive, being, 154
problem solving, 54, 60, 87, 89
procedural understanding/mastery, 88, 90, 92, 96, 97, 104, 107
project-based learning, 54, 67–68
projects. *See also specific projects*
   in discovery learning approach, 58–59, 60
   organizing time for, 143–144
   prevalence of, 10
   students as opting to complete easiest option, 78, 79
   writing-centred projects, 46
provincial exams, preparation for, 204
Psychological Science in the Public Interest, 75
punctuation, 9, 46, 47, 64, 80
"Putting Students on the Path to Learning: The Case for Fully Guided Instruction" (Clark, Kirschner, and Sweller), 56

Q

quick and easy worksheets, 155
quizzes
   as more and more rare, 10
   surprise quizzes and students who are proactive, 154

R

reading
- aloud, 159
- learning to read as not a natural process, 112, 125
- looking at questions first in reading assignment, 160
- parent's role in their child's mastery of, 124–127
- path to mastery in, 118–124
- skim-reading, 156, 157–158
- teaching of, 111–129

Reading Research Quarterly, 119
reading responses, 67–68
reflective exercises, 117
religious beliefs, 25, 182
repetition
- importance of, 101, 155
- of material from grade to grade, 47–50
- purpose of, 90
- students' reluctance to follow advice that involves, 154

report cards, 11–12, 152, 208
responsibility, as intangible, 164, 165–166
retention, 17
retests, 10
reviewing (studying process), 151–152
reviewing material, from prior grade, 45
Rohrer, Doug, 75
routines, establishing, 150–153
rubrics, 10
Russell, Deb, 94

S

SATs, preparation for, 203
Saxon Math, 106, 107
school day, length of, 34
school-based programs, for academic help, 212–214
The Schools We Need and Why We Don't Have Them (Hirsch), 57
The Science of Reading: A Handbook (Nation), 120
The Science of Reading (Snow and Juel), 115
self-assessments, 10
self-confidence, 17, 75, 169
self-control, 169
self-directed learning, 54
self-esteem
- allure of, 4–7
- as focus of teacher-education programs, 28, 29–30
- impact of society's focus on, 164
- and learning styles, 75–76
- real self-esteem, 23–24
- reality of, 8–18

self-esteem movement, 1, 3–24
self-importance, 20–21
self-monitoring, 31
self-testing, 160
self-view, 20–22
self-worth, 6, 19, 24, 65, 66, 75
service words, 114
sight word (reading approach), 113–115
sight words, 113–115, 125
skim-reading, 156, 157–158
skits, 67

slide shows, 46, 56, 58, 67
small-group discussions, 117
small-group learning, 32
smartboards, 34, 35
smartphones, 134
Snider, Vicki, 82, 83
Snow, Catherine E., 115
social justice, 28–29, 163, 174, 187
social promotion, 16–18
socialization, 188–189
space, organization of, 135–138
spatial intelligence, 72
special needs, 184–185, 201–202
spelling, 9, 64, 80, 119, 159
sports, 100, 127, 140, 141, 183–184, 190–191, 201
Stahl, Steven A., 81
standards, 9, 18, 25, 39, 40, 41, 50, 214
Stout, Maureen, 15, 21
student-centred approach, 34, 51, 94, 113, 116–118. *See also* child-centred learning; learner-centred approach
students
    differences in preferences to learning, 84
    discovery-based approach as emphasizing uniqueness of, 65–66
    as guinea pigs, 2
"Students Need Challenges, Not Easy Success" (Clifford), 23
study skills, 31, 131–132, 145–146, 149–150
study spaces, 135–138

subject-specific training, for teachers, 28
subtraction, 64, 99, 103
Sweller, John, 56, 58, 69, 83

T

tablet computers, 34, 35, 134
teachable moments, 175–176
teacher, as facilitator, 34, 54, 55, 59, 100
teacher-centred classroom, 54
teacher-training programs
    as asking teachers to suspend common sense, 218
    overview, 28–30
    as saturated with discovery-based learning concepts, 62
Teaching and Learning in the Elementary School, 62
teaching approaches. *See also* philosophies in education
    authentic, 93, 94
    brain-based learning, 28
    child-centred, 54, 62
    discovery learning. *See* discovery learning
    global, 113
    hands-on learning, 54, 67, 94
    individual learning styles, 6, 71–84
    inquiry-based learning, 54
    learner-centred, 116
    look and say, 113
    one-size-fits-all, 73–74
    prior knowledge/experience, 116–117

project-based learning, 54, 67–68
self-esteem movement, 1, 3–24
sight word, 113–115
small-group learning, 32
student-centred. *See* student-centred approach
tendency to throw out current in favour of new, 27
three-cueing system, 115
whole-language reading. *See* whole-language reading approach
technology
    assumption as being widely and effectively used, 34–36
    challenge of in classroom, 35
    impact of changes in, 44
    placing of in students' hands, 35
test preparation, 141, 145, 199, 203–204
tests
    as more and more rare, 10
    outside help with, 214–215
    prevalence of retests, 10
Theory of Multiple Intelligences (MI), 72
three-cueing system (reading approach), 115
time, wasted, 45–46, 57–58
time management, 139–146
The Tipping Point (Gladwell), xiii
tolerance, 7, 163, 175, 188
tutoring, 199–200, 202–214
tutoring companies, 210–212

Twenge, Jean M., 18, 20

U

unconditional validation, 18
university
    self-esteem and success in, 15
    students' inadequate preparation for, 46–47, 99

V

videos, 35, 56, 82

W

wall calendars, 134–135
wasted time, 45–46, 57–58
What's Wrong with Our Schools and How We Can Fix Them (Zwaagstra, Clifton, and Long), 218
whiteboards, 32, 34, 134, 138
whole-language reading approach, 9, 113, 116, 117, 118, 122, 125, 129
willingness, importance of, 85
willpower, 169
Wilson, W. Stephen, 99
window for learning, 33
wisdom, as intangible, 164, 171–172
word lists, 113, 119
word problems, 54, 55, 64, 107
worksheets, quick and easy, 155
Wren, Sebastian, 114
writing
    breaking it down as tool for, 159
    essay writing, 47, 137

free writing, 9, 64
  putting process of into
    practice, 79
  students as struggling
    with basic, foundational
    concepts, 55, 56, 62
  teaching of with discovery
    approach, 64
  using brainstorming, 158
  writing-centred projects, 46
Wu, Hung-His, 90

Z
Zwaagstra, Michael C., 218

About the Author

Marc Lapointe, founder of Acumen Education, has a graduate degree in Education and has worked as an educator for the past two decades. Formerly a classroom teacher, Marc now works with families and other educators to not only help struggling students improve in school, but also to help bring a common sense approach to teaching and learning back into the classroom. Marc and his wife, Cindy, have two teenage children and live in Abbotsford, British Columbia.

Edwards Brothers Malloy
Oxnard, CA USA
September 20, 2013